# Shining in the darkness

# Shining in the darkness

## Philippians simply explained

### Michael Bentley

 **EVANGELICAL PRESS**

EVANGELICAL PRESS
Grange Close, Faverdale North Industrial Estate, Darlington,
Co. Durham, DL3 0PH, England

First published 1997

**British Library Cataloguing in Publication Data available**

ISBN 0 85234 403 1

Printed and bound in Great Britain by Creative Print and Design
Wales, Ebbw Vale.

To my three lovely grandchildren,
Daniel, Benjamin and Amy Felts,
with my prayer that they will all grow up
knowing much of the joy of the Lord

# Contents

# Foreword

Many believers are bemused by the mass of new Christian literature appearing month by month on church bookstalls. My recommendation is to build up a selection of useful Bible commentaries, thus getting to know the ways of God better, as well as learning to test the real worth of all the other books clamouring for your attention.

Commentaries by scholarly theologians can be of great value, although more are now being published than are necessary. Most of all we need the help of those whose work is to feed, guard and care for God's people week by week. Michael Bentley is just such an experienced pastor and teacher.

It has been often noted that Paul's main prison epistles (Ephesians, Philippians and Colossians) have remarkable qualities. Chained he might be, yet this joyful prisoner of the Lord never wrote more warmly nor more wisely than in this letter to his friends in Philippi. He so greatly valued their generous 'partnership' with him in his labours, both by praying and giving. Yet the apostle is not blind to faults, even of loyal brethren for whom he has a special affection. Evidently there was some dissension in this lively Christian community, due to personal jealousies and animosities. Unfortunately the same can be just as true today. The gospel is still at times preached from motives of selfish ambition and rivalry. All of us are still inclined to look after our own interests only. And fine Christian workers, like Euodia and Syntyche, are still quarrelling. So the call to work out our salvation with fear and trembling is still valid. Be warned by this letter; be guided by it, and be refreshed by it.

Dick Lucas

# Preface

For sixteen years I taught Religious Education at a local comprehensive school. In July 1997 my wife and I were among a large number present at a gathering to mark the school's twenty-fifth birthday and to say farewell to two long-serving, senior members of staff. One of these, who was taking early retirement, partly on health grounds, told me that he had appreciated the letters that I had sent him on two different occasions when he had been ill. I often try to write to people in such circumstances, but, because I tend to write several letters one after the other, I am aware that often they are rather rushed and my handwriting becomes difficult to read.

In one sense Paul's epistle to the Philippians was basically a 'thank you' letter from the apostle to his friends expressing appreciation for the gift they had sent him when they learned he was in prison (1:5; 4:10-19). But it was much more than that. It was not something 'dashed off quickly', like the kind of thing I tend to produce when I am answering a pile of letters.

This letter is different from Paul's other epistles, yet it is still rich in doctrinal and practical truth. Unlike others, this letter does not contain any quotation from the Old Testament. Another notable feature is that it is characterized by joy. This is a recurring theme, as the apostle speaks of his own joy and encourages his readers to rejoice with him. However, the epistle to the Philippians is no lightweight note. Indeed, it contains one of the most profound Christological passages in the New Testament (2:5-11). Yet even these verses, so rich in theological content, are placed within the framework of very practical demands for Christian living.

As I meet believers from different churches, one of the things that concerns me is that there is a tendency today among God's people to be full of complaints. Even though they are true Christians, so many have still not taken note of the lessons taught to the Israelites during their wanderings in the desert (e.g. Exod. 16:2,6-8); nor have they learned to be content, whatever their outward circumstances (Phil. 4:11). The difficulties of this life and the depravity of the world around them have affected God's people far more than they are prepared to admit.

One of my longings is that all believers should have the burning desire and determination to seek, to the very best of their ability, to live holy lives and, as a consequence, to shine like stars in the darkness of this world, as they use all of their energies to hold out the word of life (Phil. 2:15-16).

This book is based on a series of Sunday morning sermons preached to the congregation of Great Hollands Free Church between October 1995 and May 1996. Our study of this epistle showed us what true joy is and helped us to see how we should live out our faith, despite the apathy and ungodliness of the large housing estate where we worship and witness.

I want to place on record my gratitude to the very many people who have supported me in studying this letter and preaching through it. Particularly I want to thank the staff of Evangelical Press who have been very patient with me when I have not explained myself clearly enough and have also made numerous suggestions for the improvement of my manuscript.

My prayer is that these pages will be a challenge to all of us, so that 'whatever happens, [we may] conduct [ourselves] in a manner worthy of the gospel of Christ' (Phil. 1:27).

Michael Bentley
November 1997

# 1.
# Joyful people

*Please read Philippians 1:1-2*

What do you do when you receive a letter and you do not recognize the handwriting on the envelope? The first thing I do is to open it and try to find the last page to see who has signed it. However, when they wrote letters in ancient Rome, instead of burying the signature right near the end of the letter, they started off with it. This is why most of the letters in the New Testament start with the word **'Paul'**. The name of the writer was always followed by the names of those to whom the letter was addressed; after that there would be a short greeting.

## The writer of this letter

This letter was written by the apostle Paul to his dear Christian friends at Philippi. He was clearly in prison at the time because 1:13 tells us that he is 'in chains for Christ'. Even though he was imprisoned, he still wrote a cheerful letter to his friends. They were obviously anxious about him, yet this letter overflows with joy. In one form or another, the words 'joy' and 'rejoice' occur some sixteen times in the space of four chapters.

God intended this letter to be a message to *all of God's people*, down through the ages until today — and beyond. The Lord wants us *all* to share in the experience of Christian joy.

Paul was glad that he could share in the sufferings of Christ. Jesus spoke to his disciples just before his betrayal and said, 'I have told you [about my coming death] so that my joy may be in you and that your joy may be complete' (John 15:11). The reason the Lord experienced such delight was because he knew he was obeying his Father's will. Paul felt the same in his trials.

**'Timothy'** is also mentioned alongside of Paul. This was because Timothy was with Paul, and the believers at Philippi knew him. Indeed, he had lived and worked among them for some long time. The apostle describes both Timothy and himself as **'servants of Christ Jesus'** (1:1). Unlike in other letters, Paul does not describe himself as an apostle. He evidently did not feel it necessary to emphasize the power and authority which the Lord had given him because he and the Philippians loved and respected each other.

### The recipients of this letter

Paul addresses his letter to **'all the saints in Christ Jesus at Philippi'** (1:1). He seems reluctant to single out any specific group in the church. In verse 4 he says that his prayers are for '*all* of you'; in verses 7 and 8 he speaks of his affection for '*all* of you'; and in verse 25 he tells them that he is interested in the progress of '*all* of you'.

He calls them 'saints' — a word which he often uses to describe Christian believers. This word means 'those who are set apart', and he uses it because they had been set apart for God's glory and separated from the world and all its contamination. However, this did not absolve them from the responsibility to preach the gospel to every person.

Paul also says that they are 'in Christ Jesus'. This is because all believers, in every age, have been blessed 'with every spiritual blessing *in Christ*' (Eph. 1:3). If we are real Christians, then Christ lives in us. In Acts 16 we can read about the foundation of this church to whom Paul is writing. When he commenced his letter, **'Paul and Timothy, servants of Christ Jesus, to all the saints in Christ Jesus at Philippi, together with the overseers and deacons...'** (1:1), he would have thought of Lydia and the jailer and the slave girl, and so many others whom we know nothing about — except that they were 'in Christ Jesus' and 'at Philippi'.

## The benefits of living at Philippi

The citizens of Philippi were proud of their Greek history. Philippi had been founded by the famous Greek king Philip of Macedon, father of Alexander the Great. He had established the city at that place mainly because of the gold which was being mined there. But several hundreds of years later, when Paul and his friends arrived at Philippi for the first time, Rome was the dominant power in the area.

The Roman Empire was famous for its straight roads. One of these was the *Via Egnatia*, which stretched all the way from the Adriatic Sea (to the east of Italy) to the Aegean Sea (to the south-east of Greece). Anyone who travelled along that road from Rome to the eastern province of Asia (now called Turkey) would have had to pass through the city of Philippi.

## The privileges of Roman citizenship

Philippi was designated as a Roman colony, even though it was a long way from the city of Rome. While its citizens were proud of their Greek history, they also gloried in their status as Roman citizens. Philippi was 'a Rome in miniature, a reproduction on a small scale of the imperial city'.[1] As Roman citizens, the inhabitants enjoyed all the rights of Roman citizens everywhere. This meant that they could not be scourged, or arrested (except in extreme cases) and they had a right to appeal directly to the emperor if they were not satisfied with the way they were treated by any official. That is why the magistrates were so worried when they eventually found out that Paul and Silas were Roman citizens. They knew that they were breaking Roman law by flogging them and putting them in prison without a proper trial (Acts 16:38).

However, because the Philippians had the status of Roman citizens, it was necessary that they should behave as Romans. For instance, they spoke Latin, instead of Greek. The coins which they used bore Latin inscriptions. They dressed in the Roman style of clothing and they enjoyed the many benefits that citizenship of that city-state conferred — e.g. exemption from paying tribute to Rome, the right to acquire, hold and transfer property and freedom from interference by the provincial governor. If they were retired Roman soldiers, then they also received a grant of land from the emperor. Naturally, they were justly proud of their status as Greek people who lived in a Roman colony.

In this letter Paul makes several references to the citizenship of the Philippians. In 1:27 he tells them to behave as citizens and in 3:20 he reminds his readers that 'Our citizenship is in heaven.'

## The blessings of dual citizenship

The Philippians enjoyed all the privileges of Roman citizenship, but because they lived in Greece they literally had the best of both worlds. They knew that if things became difficult they could appeal directly to Cæsar for help, and they had magistrates to protect them from injustices.

Because of the Philippians' knowledge about Rome and its system of government, Paul did not need to explain to them what the praetorian guard was. These were the members of 'the palace guard' (1:13).

Later in the letter, Paul speaks of another kind of dual citizenship which his readers also enjoyed and reminds them of the responsibilities which this laid upon them. He writes, 'Whatever happens, conduct yourselves in a manner worthy of the gospel of Christ' (1:27). They would have remembered how he and Silas had conducted themselves when they were wrongfully arrested, beaten and thrown into prison (see Acts 16:22-24). They did not complain. They just behaved as citizens — not of Rome, but of the kingdom of heaven. They were glad to suffer shame for the sake of the gospel. No doubt they remembered the words of the Lord when he said, 'Rejoice and be glad, because great is your reward in heaven, for in the same way they persecuted the prophets who were before you' (Matt. 5:12).

Paul goes on to tell the Philippians, 'Our citizenship is in heaven. And we eagerly await a Saviour from there, the Lord Jesus Christ, who, by the power that enables him to bring everything under his control, will transform our lowly bodies so that they will be like his glorious body' (3:20-21). In other words, Paul is telling his readers, 'Although you are proud of your dual citizenship, you must remember that you have an even greater dual citizenship.'

## The leaders of the church at Philippi

The New International Version of the Bible translates the names for these leaders as **'overseers and deacons'** (1:1). In Greek the word for 'overseer' is *'episkopos'*, which literally means 'one who watched over' (a footnote in the NIV gives the alternative reading, 'traditionally "bishops"'). Church dignitaries who are called 'bishops' in the Anglican or Roman Catholic Churches bear little resemblance to the overseers Paul is writing about here. In New Testament times it is evident that there were a number of overseers in each congregation who had specific responsibilities. In Acts 20:17,28 we see that these people are called both 'elders' and 'overseers'. Both of these words are used to refer to the same people.

The overseers were joined in leadership by those who were called 'deacons'. This is the only one of Paul's letters which is addressed to both overseers and deacons. He outlines the responsibilities of overseers and deacons in 1 Timothy 3 and Titus 1. There he tells us that the overseers have the task of leading the church in spiritual ways, while the deacons have the duty to lead the church in more practical matters. Both types of leaders came from the membership of the church and there was more than one overseer and deacon for each congregation. It is for that reason that Paul writes, **'To all the saints in Christ Jesus at Philippi, together with the overseers and deacons'** (1:1). He did not write, 'to all the saints ... *under* the overseers and deacons'. Neither did he say, 'to all the saints ... *after* the overseers and deacons'. He was concerned to show that every church member has a part to play in the church. Leaders should have due respect shown to them and are to be obeyed, but they are not more important than the humblest church member.

### The greeting

**'Grace and peace to you from God our Father and the Lord Jesus Christ'** (1:2). Paul gave this same greeting in six of his other letters (Rom. 1:7; 1 Cor. 1:3; 2 Cor. 1:2; Gal. 1:3; Eph. 1:2; Philem. 3). He also uses very similar words in 2 Thessalonians 1:2. He tells us that both grace and peace come from God our Father and the Lord Jesus Christ.

The word 'grace' has a very wide range of meanings, all of which are demonstrated in God's free, unmerited favour to men and women who deserve his wrath. Paul's writings are full of this term and he gives an extended explanation of it in Romans 3:21 - 4:25. When we speak of the grace of God we mean his many-faceted kindness which he has granted to us. Paul writes to the Corinthians, 'You know the grace of our Lord Jesus Christ, that though he was rich, yet for your sakes he became poor, so that you through his poverty might become rich' (2 Cor. 8:9). He also tells the Ephesians, 'To each one of us grace has been given' (Eph. 4:7). He means that through Christ's death we have been delivered from the guilt of our sins and we have been given a guarantee of entrance into heaven when we die.

The other desire which Paul expressed for his friends was that they should experience God's 'peace'. God's grace ought to bloom in our lives and grant us peace. Like the word 'grace', 'peace' was often on the believer's lips. Indeed, the Hebrew word for peace, *'Shalom'*, was — and still is — used constantly as a greeting by all Jews whenever they met one another.

God sent his Son to grant us salvation, but along with that salvation he gave us grace, and this grace leads us to have peace in our hearts. We have peace because we have been reconciled to God through Christ. Hendriksen puts it like this: 'Grace is the fountain, and peace is the stream which issues from the fountain.'[2] Or, as Ralph Martin says, 'Peace is the fruit of God's gracious activity in the experience of sinners.'[3]

We read of two main kinds of peace in the Bible. There is peace *with* God. Paul tells the Romans, 'Since we have been justified through faith, we have peace with God through our Lord Jesus Christ' (Rom. 5:1). All those who have truly been born again have peace with God. They know that they have sinned in God's sight, and they realize that they continue to do so, yet they have the assurance within their hearts and consciences that Christ has taken away their sins. There is now no barrier between them and God. Therefore, they have peace with God.

We also read about the peace *of* God. This is something which is experienced by the believer who is undergoing trials of one kind or another. When Paul was fastened in the stocks at Philippi on his first visit to the city, he could still sing praises to God although he had been badly beaten. This was because he had the peace of God. Countless saints have experienced this same calmness of mind and spirit. Paul told these Philippians that the peace of God, which transcends all understanding, would guard their hearts and minds in Christ Jesus (4:7).

# 2.
# Joyful memories

*Please read Philippians 1:3-6*

Memory is a wonderful thing. I have heard it said that a computer, even one the size of a large office block, would not be anything like large enough to contain the huge amount of information which is stored up in just one human brain. Something triggers off a thought in the brain and all the memories come flooding back — especially of those things which happened when we were children.

Paul must have recalled some bad things about Philippi, but his most dominant memories of the believers in that place were happy ones.

## Happy memories

Every time the apostle remembered his friends at Philippi he was filled with joy — so much so that he thanked his God for each one of the believers there. He tells them, **'I thank my God every time I remember you. In all my prayers for all of you, I always pray with joy'** (1:3-4). Paul knew them all. He had been there when many of them had first come to know the Lord as their Saviour, and because of this he could pray for each one of them by name. Obviously there must have been others added to the church during the ten years or so since he had last visited them, but he knew enough about what was happening at Philippi to be able to pray for them all.

Warren Wiersbe suggests that we should all ask ourselves, 'Am I the kind of person who brings joy to my pastor's mind when he thinks of me?'[1] Paul never had any trouble wondering what to pray about when he thought of his friends. When he settled down to pray for the church at Philippi he did not just pray for the overseers and deacons (the leaders of the church); he prayed for all the saints who were at Philippi — even the most insignificant believer (1:1). He thought of each one and pleaded at the throne of God on behalf of the particular needs of all the members of that church.

Paul would have remembered various believers at Philippi. He would not have forgotten *Lydia*, whose heart the Lord opened. She was one of the first believers at Philippi. This lady had a business brain; she was rich and well organized. When she became a Christian the Lord opened up her heart to receive his salvation. After she was converted she opened up her home for the use of the gospel workers (Acts 16:14,15), and she continued to keep it open for all who would come (Acts 16:40).[2]

Before she was converted, Lydia may have been particular about whom she invited to her home, but when Christ entered her life she was transformed. She handed over everything to him — not just her life, but her home and business as well. That is what happens to us when we are born again: we become a new creation. It is not surprising that Paul thanked God for the believers at Philippi. He saw the grace of God at work in their lives and the evidence that they were changing to become more like Christ himself.

Paul would also have remembered *the Philippian jailer*. This man was quite the opposite of gentle Lydia. He had, in all probability, been a Roman soldier — and a tough one at that! Certainly as a jailer he had learned to harden himself to witness some appalling punishments. He may even have instigated some of them himself and personally taken part in the whipping of prisoners. At any rate, it does seem that he had handled Paul and Silas very roughly. Luke tells us that after they had been flogged they were thrown into prison. It was this jailer himself who had 'put them into the inner cell and fastened their feet in the stocks' (Acts 16:22-24). As he did so, he must have noticed their bleeding and battered backs, but evidently did nothing about them. Yet, through the preaching of the gospel, this hardened soldier had been completely changed.

Paul, of all people, knew what this man had been like before his conversion, but now he could testify that the jailer was a new man in Christ. After his conversion, instead of handling Paul and Silas roughly, he had tenderly washed their wounds and placed food before them (Acts 16:33-34). No wonder that Paul could thank his God every time he remembered this man! Despite his former behaviour, Paul could honestly pray with joy every time he remembered him.

It was not only Lydia and the jailer who gave Paul cause for thanksgiving; he thanked God for all of the believers. We do not know the names of the others, or anything about most of them, but Paul did. And, much more important, so did the Lord.

The Philippian church must have been a lovely gathering. I am sure it was not without its problems, or its awkward people (see 4:2), but Paul loved each one of them. He could say, 'In *all my prayers for all of you*, I always pray with joy' (1:4). 'It is right for me to feel this way about *all of you*' (1:7). 'God can testify how I long for *all of you*' (1:8) and 'I rejoice with *all of you*' (2:17).

## Memories of partnership

Paul was not only filled with joy because he had happy memories of them all. He could also joyfully pray for them because of their work, together with him, in spreading and teaching the gospel message. They had not been slackers. Nothing put them off from telling others about the Lord Jesus Christ. They were so blessed by their new relationship with Christ that they wanted everyone else to enjoy that same fellowship with God which they had.

Their work was not drudgery to them because it was based on love. They had a deep love for the Lord. After all, without him they would have had nothing of real value. He had hung and suffered and died on the cross to take away their sins and give them new life. If they had not appreciated God's grace Paul could never have written to them, **'God can testify how I long for all of you with the affection of Christ Jesus'** (1:8).

They also had a deep love for Paul, and for others who taught them the Word of God. Paul knew this and he in turn could say, **'I have you in my heart'** (1:7). We know that they loved him and he loved them for the sake of the gospel and of Christ. One of the marks of true Christians is that they love one another. John wrote, 'This is the message you heard from the beginning: We should love one another' (1 John 3:11). He also said, 'We know that we have passed from death to life, because we love our brothers' (1 John 3:14). This was the command of the Lord himself: 'A new command I give you: Love one another. As I have loved you, so you must love one another. By this all men will know that you are my disciples, if you love one another' (John 13:34).

It was for these and many other reasons that Paul could say, **'I thank my God every time I remember you. In all my prayers for all of you, I always pray with joy because of your partnership in the gospel from the first day until now'** (1:4-5).

It is a sign of Christian love when church members invite others to a meal, especially after a morning service in church. It is an indication of warm fellowship when one believer telephones another to cheer him or her up, or sends a helpful letter or cheerful greetings card to someone who is lonely, depressed — or maybe full of joy. This is demonstrating what Paul enjoined the Corinthian believers to do. If one part of the body of Christ (i.e. the believers) suffers, then each of the others should suffer with that one; and if one believer is honoured, then all should share in that honour (1 Cor. 12:26)

These Philippians had also taken an active part in spreading the gospel. They had *prayed* for Paul and his work. In the same way Christians today should take a warm interest in those on the mission-field. These believers in Philippi prayed hard for the success of the gospel and *gave money* for those who worked at spreading the good news. One of the reasons why Paul wrote this letter was to thank them for their financial help in the work. 'It was good of you to share in my troubles,' he said, 'Not one church shared with me in the matter of giving and receiving, except you only; for even when I was in Thessalonica, you sent me aid again and again when I was in need' (4:14,16).

They also *worked* in spreading the gospel. They even sent one of their members to help Paul in his evangelism and to care for his needs (2:25). His name was Epaphroditus. Paul calls him his 'brother, fellow-worker and fellow-soldier'. The apostle also describes Euodia, Syntyche, Clement and others as 'those who have contended at my side in the cause of the gospel' (4:2-3).

## Memories of persistence

Paul saw their partnership in the gospel as an evidence that they were true Christians. Having started well, he had no doubt that they would continue in the Christian faith. Sometimes we have doubts about our faith, particularly when we think about the Day of Judgement which is coming on the world — or our own death. We ask ourselves, 'Am I a true Christian?'

Sometimes the devil says to us, 'You are too wicked to be saved.' Or he asks, 'What makes you so big-headed that you think that God has time to take notice of you?' Then he tries a different tack and challenges us by telling us, 'It is all a delusion. There is no life after death. Everyone will just fade away into oblivion.'

Paul would have none of that kind of talk or thinking. He was confident that these Philippians had been saved from the wrath to come, and he knew that they were safe for evermore. He had good grounds for assurance about these believers.

First of all, *he had been present at the conversion of a number of them.* He had spoken to them about the wonderful love of God in sending his only Son down to this earth to die for sinners. He had witnessed how the Lord had opened up the heart of Lydia (Acts 16:14) and he had observed the sincere pleading in the eyes of the jailer when he had called out, in utter despair, 'Sirs, what must I do to be saved?' (Acts 16: 30).

Secondly, *Paul had seen how they continued to live out the Christian faith.* He had witnessed the enthusiasm with which they entered into the work of spreading the good news and he thanked God for their partnership in the gospel. Because of all this, he was confident that God had started his work of salvation in their lives. This is what he means by saying, **'He who began a good work in you...'** (1:6).

He had seen evidences of the working of the Holy Spirit in the lives of each of these Philippian believers. He had witnessed the fact that, even before they had confessed Christ publicly, God was at work in their hearts and consciences. God's good work can never fail. He has planned the salvation of each child of God in Christ before the creation of the world; and what he purposes he brings to full fruition. That is why Paul could say that he who began a good work in them **'will**

**carry it on to completion until the day of Christ Jesus'**
(1:6). The work of God in the life of a sinner is the only activity
which can bring a person to heaven.

Paul was confident that God would carry on this work. The
evidence of that was the great enthusiasm these believers had
for the work of the gospel. They did not falter when the work
became hard. They did not flag when they became tired of
witnessing to the truth. They did not give up when they met
with opposition and lack of success. They kept on keeping on,
and God also continued this good work within their souls.

Paul was confident, not only that God would care for them,
but that the Lord would bring them safely to 'the day of Christ
Jesus'. By that phrase he meant 'the end of time'. He was
talking about the Day of Judgement when all the books will be
opened and we shall all be judged on how we have lived.

Paul was confident that the names of each of these believers
had been written clearly in the book of life. He writes about
that in 4:3. There is no suggestion that God just pencils in our
names until he sees how things will work out. When God
writes your name in his book, it is there for ever.

Sometimes the devil tempts troubled Christians to question
whether they are real believers and their names really are
written in God's book. The way to counter that evil insinuation
of Satan is for these people to make sure that they have truly
repented of their sins and trusted in Christ's shed blood to wash
them away. They should also tell the Evil One that God never
uses pencil or washable ink to record the names of those who
are his! In fact, he does not use ink at all. When the people of
Israel thought that God had forgotten them he replied, 'I will
not forget you! See, I have engraved you on the palms of my
hands' (Isa. 49:15-16). Anyone would have a tough job trying
to rub out engraving!

Paul knew that God would continue to work in the lives of
these believers and bring them safely to heaven. This is why

he thanked God and rejoiced every time he remembered them. He also thanked God because he knew that he would see them again, if not in Philippi, then in heaven. He did not know whether he would soon be executed or not, but he was sure that if he died he would go straight to be with God in heaven (1:21).

All of these things gave him great joy. He knew that, whatever happened to him, or his friends, they were all in God's hands, which is the very best place for anyone to be.

# 3.
# Genuine longing

*Please read Philippians 1:7-11*

When we, in our day, want to communicate with our friends, we can do so by letter (as Paul did) but we can also use other means to reach our acquaintances. We can telephone them, or fax them, or send them an e-mail. However, if the people we are trying to contact do not want to hear from us, then there are things which they can do to stop our message reaching them. They can ignore us. They can refuse to open our letters. They can put the phone down on us when we ring them, and they can pay no attention to our faxes or e-mails.

But there is one means of communication which no one can prevent us from using, and that is prayer. People can tell us that they do not want to hear from us. They can refuse to talk to us, but they can never stop us from praying for them. When we pray for someone we can be sure that our message reaches our heavenly Father (providing there is no sin in our lives which is blocking the way). Our messages cannot be intercepted or diverted by anyone. There is nothing which can delay them, or diminish their impact, or prevent their acceptance, because God always hears and answers prayer.

In this chapter I want us to see what we can learn about prayer, by examining very carefully the kind of thing for which Paul prayed in verses 9-11.

**Paul had the Philippians in his heart**

The apostle tells his readers, **'It is right for me to feel this way about all of you, since I have you in my heart'** (1:7). This was because he was bound up with them. He was so taken up with them that he could not stop praying for them. Every time he thought about them his heart was drawn out in prayer for them, and he was filled with joy as he prayed for them, because he knew that they were one with him in the grace of God (1:7).

Paul had no doubt that their lives were completely dedicated to the Lord and his service. So every time he remembered them, he recalled evidences that they belonged to the Lord and he was convinced that they would never tire of their devotion to God. He was certain that God had begun his good, saving work in their lives, and he knew that the Lord would continue with that new life within them. He knew also that when Jesus comes again, on **'the day of Christ'** (1:6,10), then they would still be faithful followers of the Lord.

Paul also knew that it was right that he should feel like that about the Philippians (1:7). He could have been excused if he had allowed his circumstances to prevent him from feeling like this about them. After all, he was in prison and he had been confined there for no good reason. But he was not bitter with the Lord. He never complained, 'Why did you call me to such a great work and then allow me to be shut up away from those whom you want me to serve?' Nor did he ask, 'How can you be a God of love and yet do such a thing?' He allowed no recriminations of this type to stop his heart going out to the believers at Philippi.

Have you ever thought what it must have been like for those prisoners of war who were shut up in Japanese prison camps in the Far East during the war? Very many of them were so badly treated, and deprived of food and medical care, that we could forgive them for being so taken up with their own conditions as to have no thought for anyone else. However, I imagine that uppermost in their minds was a deep longing and desire for their families at home.

Although Paul was in a similar situation, there was nothing which could prevent him longing for his dear Christian friends. He said that it was only right and natural for him to feel concern for their well-being. However bad his circumstances were, he still had them in his heart.

One of the reasons why he felt such love for them was that he knew of their very real concern for his welfare. They cared so much for him that it was as though they were sitting with him in his damp prison cell or standing next to him in court when he was **'defending and confirming the gospel'** (1:7). Indeed, the fact that they suffered with him, even though they were many miles away, showed Paul that they were all sharing in God's grace with him. They were partakers both of his discomfort and his declaration of Christ, and they were beneficiaries of the same grace of God which was his.

### Paul had them in his affections

The apostle continues, **'God can testify how I long for all of you with the affection of Christ Jesus'** (1:8). It is possible to have certain people in our minds, but not in our affections. We may tell them we are thinking about them. We have a natural concern about them and we do not want to see them hurt, even if we do not particularly like them. But we do not go around telling them that we love them. If we did that to all and sundry, people would think that there was something wrong with us. We left the age of 'flower power' thirty years ago, and that kind of talk seems a little hollow and insincere in these days. When we speak of loving someone we are usually talking about a very special feeling.

In English we only have one word for love, but there are four different Greek words for love. In popular songs this word 'love' is banded around a great deal. When singers sing about love, they are referring to the earthly kind of love which is characterized by that little boy with the bow and arrow in Piccadilly Circus in London, Eros (whose name is the Greek word for sexual love).

But there is another Greek word, *philio,* which means 'family love'. This is the kind of love we show to our relations. When I taught Religious Education in a comprehensive school I used to explain the difference between these two words by saying, 'You don't kiss your granny in the same way that you kiss your girl friend.'

However, there is a special kind of Christian love which is completely different from, and over and above, both these other kinds of love. This is the love which God demonstrated when he sent his Son to this earth to die on the cross for his people. It is this *agape* love which Paul is writing about here, and in so many other places in the New Testament.

## Paul had them in his prayers

The first thing that Paul prayed for was that their **'love'** should **'abound more and more'** (1:9). He wanted to see evidence that Christian love was increasing among them. Indeed, he desired that their love would grow more and more each day. His concern was that it should be as persistent as the waves on the seashore; he longed to know that their love was continuing to roll in time after time with nothing being able to hamper its flow or diminish its progress. And not only that — he prayed that their love would keep on growing richer and fuller all the time.

Now this is not something which we can just sit down and try to achieve like a New Year's resolution. It is something for which the grace and help of God are required. That is why Paul writes to the church at Thessalonica, 'May the Lord make your love increase and overflow for each other and for everyone else, just as ours does for you' (1 Thess. 3:12).

Nor is love something which just floats in the air, as it were. It can only be experienced when it acts.[1] God showed his love for us when he sent his Son into this world to save us from the guilt and power of our sins. The believers in Thessalonica were also demonstrating that kind of love. Paul could say of them, 'Your faith is growing more and more, and the love every one of you has for each other is increasing' (2 Thess. 1:3). In the same way Paul longed to see the Christians at Philippi showing such love, and to see it growing more and more as the days went by.

A believer should first of all show love to God. That is where the source of love is. If someone truly loves God, then he, or she, will seek to love other people as God loves him. He will never say, 'I couldn't love that person. He is so ugly, or difficult to get on with.' He will remember that God loves him, with all his faults and failings. So he will say to himself, 'I must love my fellow believers, just as God loves me.'

However, the Lord also desires that we should show love to those who are, as yet, outside of the kingdom. After all, God so loved the world that he gave his only Son. We should love the people of the world like that too. We should want to go out in Christ's name and seek to lead them to faith in God.

Paul's prayer was that he would see and hear further evidence that the Philippians were showing more and more love and that their love should abound. He desired that it should be so abundant and vigorous that it could not be held down. But he also wanted their love to be directed. He did not want it to be aimless. He longed that it should flow like a river, kept in control by two banks.[2] These banks are, on the one hand, **'knowledge'**, and on the other, **'depth of insight'** (1:9). He did not want their love to gush all over the place in an uncontrolled manner, so that they loved the wrong things. He did not want them to love the world (see 1 John 2:15-17), or money (see 1 Tim. 6:10). Nor did he want any of God's people to love themselves (James 5:5).

Paul's earnest desire for them was that they would have full and complete knowledge of God and his Word. His prayer was that their love should **'abound more and more in knowledge and depth of insight'** (1:9). Our love must be rooted in knowledge of God, and that is found by reading and meditating on the Bible. Paul desired that the Philippians should be able to exercise full discernment, so that they could tell right from wrong. We too can only have such insight as we study God's Word and apply it to the whole of our lives.

A second thing that Paul prayed for was that they should be **'able to discern what is best'** (1:10). It was not sufficient for them to be able to tell right from wrong. They needed to be able to weigh up matters so carefully that they would only choose the very best. God is never satisfied with second best. In the Old Testament anyone who brought an animal for sacrifice which was past its prime was guilty of treating God contemptuously (Mal. 1:6-13).

The reason why Paul wanted the Philippians to be able to choose the best was so that they would be **'pure and blameless until the day of Christ'** (1:10). Purity is something which we should all desire throughout our Christian lives. Occasionally we do have very pure and holy thoughts and sometimes these desires manifest themselves in kind deeds. But the purity of our lives should not just come upon us from time to time. It should be something which permeates the whole of our lives until the day of Christ (that means, when he comes to reign supremely over all things).

Paul also prayed that his friends would be 'blameless'. He meant that they should be kept from doing anything which could contaminate them. Holy living is both positive and negative. We should always seek to do those things which are right and good, and we should refrain from doing those things which are sinful and evil.

Finally, Paul prays that they might be **'filled with the fruit of righteousness that comes through Jesus Christ — to the glory and praise of God'** (1:11). Fruit is what a tree or plant produces at harvest-time. A farmer only keeps a fruit tree if it gives him a good crop. Paul wanted to see much good coming to others through the lives of his readers. He wanted them to serve God with humility. When a fruit tree produces its crop, it does so without a great deal of noise.[3] In the same way, Paul does not want the Philippians to make a big show of their goodness. Nevertheless he does pray that the good deeds which they do will bring great glory to God's name.

Paul wrote to the Galatians about this fruit of the Spirit. He told them that 'The fruit of the Spirit is love, joy, peace, patience, kindness, goodness, faithfulness, gentleness and self-control' (Gal. 5:22-23). If we have the Holy Spirit within us, guiding and strengthening us each day, then we shall automatically produce fruit for God's honour and glory. We shall not be controlled by selfish desires, nor shall we love things which are unhelpful for us. Our lives will be lived for the glory and praise of God. This means that there will be things about us which will be true, noble, right, pure, lovely, admirable, excellent and praiseworthy (see 4:8).

## What this means for each of us

Each of you who are reading this book needs to examine your own life and ask yourself, 'Do I have a deep love for God and the things of God? Do I show, by the way I act, that I want to live my life for God's glory?' Those who really love God will want to obey him. He calls us all to come to him and honour him by doing what he says.

The quality of our love also needs to be assessed. Has your love for God increased at all since this time last year? Do you pray to him more often? Are your prayers more real than they used to be? Do you read the Bible more intelligently and more eagerly? Do you spend more time watching television than you do in reading good spiritual books? Do you try to put into practice what you hear in sermons and Bible Studies? And are you seeking to live a more holy life than you did last year?

How pure are you? Do you think clean thoughts? Does your imagination only lead you towards heavenly desires? Have you tried to live a blameless life? Or do you think that it does not matter whether you sin or not?

Are you wanting to be filled with the fruit of righteousness? Is pleasing God your main aim in life? Or do you put what *you* want first? Do you think more of making an impression on your friends than you do about honouring God?

Do you strive to show the blessings of God to everyone you meet? Or do you want to keep the good things of the Lord to yourself? Do you use all of your energy enjoying your times of worship in church, so that you have no time to warn your unconverted friends of the dangers of hell?

# 4.
# The preaching of Christ

*Please read Philippians 1:12-18*

Do you ever become discontented with all the responsibilities which your church membership brings you? Perhaps you look around you and see other Christians enjoying themselves, just doing what they feel like doing. If they want to stay in bed one Sunday morning then they can, because they do not have any particular duty to carry out in church. If they want to go off to a large church one Sunday, where plenty is happening, then they are free to do so because they have not put themselves under any obligation to go to their normal church. If they prefer the morning service, then they do not feel obliged to turn out in the evening, and if there is no life in the prayer meetings at their church, then they only attend if things are going wrong and they feel in need of a spiritual lift-up.

Do you sometimes envy people who can behave like that? If you do, then stop it at once and consider what we have before us in this passage. If anyone ever had grounds for feeling sorry for himself, Paul certainly had, but instead of compaining, or indulging in self-pity, he tells his readers that all these dreadful things that had happened to him had really turned out for the glory of God.

## Paul's circumstances

It seems that it had reached Paul's ears that his friends at
Philippi were eager to hear how he was faring. This is why he
writes, **'Now I want you to know, brothers, that what has
happened to me has really served to advance the gospel'**
(1:12). They were naturally anxious to know what had happened to him. But, in writing to the Philippian church, Paul
does not give them a catalogue of all the things that had
befallen him since last he met with them. The subject which
was uppermost in his mind was the preaching of the gospel.
We could paraphrase what the apostle is saying to his readers
in the following way: 'Never mind about all of the trials I have
been going through; see what has happened as a result of my
sufferings: the gospel is being advanced.'

We can learn about some of the things which had happened
to Paul if we read the closing chapters of the book of Acts. He
had been falsely accused of bringing Gentiles into the Jewish
temple at Jerusalem (Acts 21:28). He had been arrested and
held fast with two chains (Acts 21:33). He had been shipped
off to Rome because he had appealed to be heard before Cæsar
(Acts 25; 26), and he had barely escaped with his life when his
ship was wrecked off the island of Malta (Acts 27:15 - 28:1).

However, because he had not committed a flagrant crime
and he was not a political prisoner who was trying to overthrow the Roman authorities, he was allowed to be kept in his
own rented house (Acts 28:30). That was not as comfortable
as it sounds, because he had a soldier with him the whole time
and it seems that he was chained to this guard (Acts 28:16;
Eph. 6:20; Col. 4:3,18; Phil. 1:13,14). But instead of complaining about these things which had happened to him, Paul
was rejoicing that the gospel was being advanced.

This word which is translated 'advance' is a military word.
It was used of scouts who were sent out ahead of the main

army. Their job was to prepare the way so that nothing would hinder the progress of the military legions as they went out to conquer a country for their empire. These sappers would make straight roads for the main body of the troops. They would erect bridges over rivers and gorges and they would clear pathways through dense undergrowth and boulder-strewn tracks.

Paul had come to Rome with a similar mission, but things had not worked out exactly as he had planned. He had often longed to go and preach the gospel at Rome, as he had at Athens, at Ephesus and at Corinth (Acts 19:21; Rom. 15:23-24,28). 'He wanted to go as a preacher but instead he went as a prisoner.'[1] Nevertheless he was not unduly cast down by his captivity. In fact he said that these things that had happened to him had really served to advance the gospel.

Satan had certainly placed many obstructions in the way of the gospel and had erected roadblocks to hinder its progress (1 Thess. 2:18; 1 Cor. 9:12). But, just as Joseph had been used by the Lord while he was imprisoned (Gen. 39:23), so was Paul.

## Paul's guards

The apostle tells us how his imprisonment had furthered the gospel in 1:13-14. Paul did not complain about his circumstances. He had, long ago, discovered that 'In all things God works for the good of those who love him' (Rom. 8:28). He knew that God was sovereign, and well able to order things to carry out his will.

In the same way, those who genuinely seek to do what God wants them to do will never be the losers. Those who are feeling cast down about their daily employment and the situation they find themselves in should remember that God knows all about it. They should seek to honour the Lord by their life and witness. They will then discover that things will go well with them.

Paul's aim in life was not his own comfort and blessing, but the advance of the gospel. Even when people were criticizing him he said, **'The important thing is that in every way, whether from false motives or true, Christ is preached. And because of this I rejoice. Yes, and I will continue to rejoice'** (1:18).

The first way in which Paul's imprisonment advanced the gospel was through the guards who were chained to him. Every six hours the guard was changed. This meant that four different soldiers were chained to Paul in each period of twenty-four hours. These soldiers were not ordinary fighters. They were the crack troops of the empire. They were the praetorian, or **'palace guard'** (1:13). Not only were they the toughest and most highly disciplined of the men, but they were probably highly intelligent too. Think about those soldiers. During the two years of Paul's imprisonment he would have had close personal contact with dozens, if not hundreds, of different men. These soldiers would have had the opportunity to observe Paul very closely.

They would have listened to him — indeed it was their duty to do so, in case he was plotting to escape. They would have heard him praying; no doubt he often prayed out loud. They would have listened to the conversations he had with the believers who visited him so freely (Acts 28:30). We are told that he 'welcomed all who came to see him'. The soldiers would have listened as he 'preached the kingdom of God and taught about the Lord Jesus Christ' (Acts 28:31). They would have overheard as he dictated his many letters to churches and believers all over the world of those days. They would also have noticed how Paul conducted himself. They would have seen his 'patience, gentleness, courage, and unswerving loyalty to [his] inner conviction'.[2]

How did they react to all this — during those long six-hour stints they spent with Paul? Some no doubt listened to him with disdain and made fun of him, but obviously others listened with great interest because, as he told the Philippians, **'As a result** [of my imprisonment] **it has become clear throughout the whole palace guard and to everyone else that I am in chains for Christ'** (1:13).

These soldiers noticed that, even though the chains must have chafed his wrists every time he moved, they did not irritate his spirits. Instead he held up his chains and said, 'I have these for the sake of the gospel.' He was not ashamed to suffer for the sake of Christ.

### Paul's acquaintances

A second way in which Paul's imprisonment served to advance the gospel was the effect his chains had on those in Rome who were already believers. The gospel had probably spread there some fifteen years before Paul's arrival. No doubt some of those who had been won for Christ on the Day of Pentecost (Acts 2) had come from Rome. When they returned they had witnessed to their friends and formed a church right there in the heart of the empire. Certainly we know that there was a church in existence some years before Paul came to Rome, because he wrote that magnificent letter to them which we have in the New Testament.

These believers, having observed Paul's attitude to his imprisonment, would have been encouraged by it. He tells his readers at Philippi that **'Because of my chains, most of the brothers in the Lord have been encouraged to speak the word of God more courageously and fearlessly'** (1:14). They took heart from Paul's attitude to his imprisonment. They realized that if the apostle could still go on witnessing for

Christ, even though he was suffering for it, then so could they. They preached Christ **'out of good will'** and **'in love'** because they knew that Paul was in Rome **'for the defence of the gospel'** (1:15,16).

Those who witness for Christ have an effect on all other believers. Those who are weaker in the faith are encouraged by the resolve of more mature believers to preach the Word of God, whatever their circumstances or difficulties. Because someone speaks for the Lord despite his or her unhelpful personal circumstances, then others are spurred on to speak the word of God more fearlessly because of that person's faithfulness to the truth of God.

However, there were other people in Rome who reacted differently to Paul's presence. It seems that they were genuine Christians but, on the other hand, they were not very gracious towards Paul and his work. The apostle says that they were preaching Christ from the wrong motives. They were doing so **'out of envy and rivalry'** (1:15). They were preaching **'out of selfish ambition, not sincerely'**, and in order to **'stir up trouble'** for Paul in his chains (1:17).

Paul's coming had evidently 'put their noses out of joint'. Probably these men had been the main preachers in Rome until his arrival, but now Paul had come along and had stolen some of their congregation. Perhaps they had overheard some of their own church members saying things like, 'That Paul is a wonderful, Spirit-anointed preacher. I could listen to him for hours and hours without getting the slightest bit bored.'

If you are the minister of a church, it is very hard not to be jealous when you hear others being praised. But if God sends someone else along who can preach better than you, then it is time for you to step to one side and make room for that man. When John the Baptist was in prison some of his disciples came to him and told him that 'Everyone is going to Jesus' (John 3:26). They were obviously very distressed at this, but

John said, with great humility, 'He must become greater; I must become less' (John 3:30).

What fired these people who were jealous of Paul? It was selfish ambition. They wanted their own church and they were determined to run it without being questioned by anyone. They were rather like Diotrephes, of whom John writes to Gaius in his third letter, 'Diotrephes, who loves to be first, will have nothing to do with us' (3 John 9).

Not only did these church leaders want to have things all their own way, they actually used their preaching to stir up trouble for the apostle. We are not told how they caused agitation, but, quite obviously, they tried to make things as difficult for Paul as possible.

If you were Paul, how would you have reacted to such behaviour? Would you have issued a strong denunciation of them all? Or would you have gone around complaining about them to all of your friends? Paul did none of these things.

## Paul's attitude

Paul's response was to say, **'Because of this I rejoice. Yes, and I will continue to rejoice'** (1:18). He did not rejoice because he knew that this kind of behaviour would eventually lead to the downfall of these worldly Christians. He rejoiced because Christ was being preached. Even if he was preached from wrong motives, Paul still rejoiced that people were able to hear about the Lord Jesus Christ. The preaching of Christ was what mattered far more than anything else.

Even though these people were preaching Christ out of jealousy of Paul, they were still preaching Christ. 'They are exercising their ambassadorship, and are publicly and authoritatively proclaiming him as the one only name under heaven that is given among men by which we must be saved.'[3] They did not belong to the group of people whom Paul describes as 'dogs ... who do evil' (3:2). They were not those who were preaching a different gospel (Gal. 1:6), or another Jesus (2 Cor. 11:4). They were truly preaching Christ, the Son of God, who had been crucified, who had been raised from the dead and who is Lord (2 Cor. 1:19; 1 Cor. 1:23; 15:11; 2 Cor. 4:5).[4]

Throughout these verses Paul continually speaks about the gospel. His imprisonment had advanced the gospel (1:12). Everyone knew that he was in chains for Christ (1:13). He was glad that the fact that he loved Christ so much that he was prepared to suffer for Christ's sake was known and talked about 'throughout the palace guard'. The brothers had been encouraged to speak the Word of God (1:14). That was what mattered to him more than anything else (1:18). He was not interested in the word of a man being proclaimed. It was the Word of God which mattered to him more than anything else.

Paul did not say that it was only the overseers and deacons who were busy at Rome speaking the word of God. He said that the brothers in the Lord had been encouraged to speak the word of God more courageously and fearlessly because of his imprisonment. This is how each of God's people should behave, even the humblest and least educated.

# 5.
# A difficult choice

*Please read Philippians 1:19-26*

In 1961 a novel by J. Heller appeared about the Second World War. It concerned some U.S. air-force pilots on combat missions over enemy-occupied territory. The story was about one of the pilots who was so traumatized by continually flying over Nazi-occupied Italy that he feigned madness so that he could be transferred away from operational duties. The problem was that the military authorities concluded that all those who claimed to be crazy were, in fact, sane people who wanted to be discharged. The hero was then faced with a moral dilemma; whatever he chose to do, he was the loser. The title of that book has now passed into our language and this kind of dilemma is often described as 'a Catch-22 situation'.

Sometimes this kind of predicament is referred to in terms of 'being caught on the horns of a dilemma'. This comes from the word 'lemma', which means something which is taken for granted, and a double 'lemma' is called a dilemma. The picture conjured up by this phrase is that of someone facing a mad bull which is charging towards him and finding that if he tries to seize hold of one horn, the bull will simply toss him with the other.[1]

As Paul was writing this epistle he, too, was facing a dilemma. He was wondering whether it was better to die — in which case he knew that he would go straight to be with Christ

— or to carry on living, which would mean he could continue to preach the gospel and would also bring joy to his friends at Philippi and elsewhere.

He had the same kind of problem as the hero in *Catch 22*, or a man facing a charge from a mad bull — except that in Paul's case, both of the options promised blessing instead of disaster. He was so anxious about this that he almost cried out, **'What shall I choose? I do not know! I am torn between the two: I desire to depart and be with Christ, which is better by far; but it is more necessary for you that I remain in the body'** (1:22-24).

But, even though he debated the alternatives, he knew that the answer did not lay in his own hands, or even in those of his captors; the outcome rested with the Lord who controls all things.

## Paul expected to be saved

Even though he was confined to prison, and waiting to hear what the authorities were going to do with him, the apostle rejoiced. In fact, he continued to rejoice (1:18). This was because he knew that, one way or the other, he was going to be saved. He was sure that if the Romans decided to take him out of the prison and execute him, then he would go straight to be with Christ, which would be far better for him than to continue living on this earth. He was not anxious because he thought that there might be a long waiting period between the moment of his death and the time when he would stand in the presence of his beloved Lord. He knew what Jesus said to the thief dying next to him on the cross: 'Today you will be with me in paradise' (Luke 23:43).

On the other hand, Paul knew that if the verdict of the judges was that he was to be set free, then everything would also go well with him, and his release would be of great benefit to the churches. Some very dreadful things had happened to him in the years leading up to his imprisonment, but he knew that those things would turn out for his deliverance (1:19). In the same way, the things which had happened to him, and resulted in his now being in chains, had really served to advance the gospel (1:12).

Paul kept on referring to what had happened to him (1:12,19). A little later he goes on to tell his readers, 'Whatever happens, conduct yourselves in a manner worthy of the gospel' (1:27).

There were two things which made Paul certain that he would be delivered (a better translation is 'saved'). The first was that his friends at Philippi and elsewhere were praying for him. Prayer is a wonderful weapon in the hands of godly people. Someone once said, 'If your troubles are deep-seated or long-standing, try kneeling!' And A. W. Pink wrote, 'The measure of our love for others can largely be determined by the frequency and earnestness of our prayers for them.' [2]

In 1:4 Paul had said, 'In all my prayers for all of you, I always pray with joy.' Now he says that he knows they are praying for him. It is a great blessing to be able to pray for others. It is also a great comfort to know that others are praying for us when we are in deep trouble. Paul knew the value of the prayers of the believers on his behalf and he said, **'I know that through your prayers ... what has happened to me will turn out for my deliverance'** (1:19). God works mightily in answer to the intercessions of his holy people.

The second factor which Paul knew would lead to his deliverance was **'the help given by the Spirit of Jesus Christ'** (1:19). The apostle knew that God does not do just whatever we ask him to do, merely because we want him to do it. When we pray we need to ask in accordance with God's will, but our prayers and desires also need the aid and support of the

Holy Spirit to carry them out. In this verse Paul calls the Holy
Spirit 'the Spirit of Jesus Christ'. There is only one Holy Spirit
and it is this same Holy Spirit of whom Paul writes here. The
Holy Spirit endued Jesus with all that was necessary for his
work on earth (see Isa. 11:1-2; 61:1-3; Matt. 3:16; John 3:34;
Heb. 9:14), and Paul says that this same Spirit of Jesus would
deliver him.[3]

Whatever happened to him, Paul wanted Christ to be
exalted in his body. He eagerly expected that he would not be
ashamed when he heard the verdict of the court (1:20). When
he wrote those words it was as though he was craning his neck
to catch a glimpse of what lay ahead of him.[4] His goal was that
Christ's glory should be seen by everyone, whatever happened
to him. His concern was that he should **'in no way be
ashamed'**, and that he would have **'sufficient courage'** to
persevere, regardless of any future events — whether he
carried on living or was put to death.

Faced with this dilemma, he made this wonderful declaration: **'For to me, to live is Christ and to die is gain'** (1:21).
He may have been hurt by the selfish way in which some
people in Rome had been preaching Christ, but his own
preaching was not self-centred; it was Christ-centred. Paul
was giving a personal testimony of what Christ meant to him.
He goes on to explain more on this theme later in this letter. We
can see from 4:13 that he knew that he derived his strength
from Christ. For Paul to live was Christ, in the sense that he
sought to have the humble attitude of Christ (2:5-11), that he
wanted to know Christ more and better (3:8,10) and that he
longed to be covered by Christ's righteousness (3:9).

**Paul looked forward to heaven**

He did not say he looked forward to death. That would be an
awful thing to say, because death is God's judgement on sin.

Nevertheless death is something which will come to all of us, unless Christ comes back to this earth before we die.

We try not to think about dying, especially when we are young. Yet it cannot be ignored for ever. Paul is not saying that we should dwell on death — certainly not if we are believers in the Lord Jesus Christ. If we know the Lord as our own personal Saviour then we have nothing to fear from death because it is the gateway into the presence of God.

So, while Christians should never look forward to death (which speaks of pain, sorrow and separation), they should look forward to heaven. This is why Paul did not fear the executioner's sword. He knew that the pain would be short and bitter, but he also knew that eternity would last for ever and would be joyful and blessed. In fact, if the message came that he was to be executed, then for him to die would be gain.

By saying that death would be gain for him, Paul meant that he would leave behind all of the cares, pain and sorrow of this world. These things would be taken from him. He would know that his work on earth had been completed. He would have the assurance that God had others who would take over from him, and carry on the work, and he would be able to die in peace, knowing that God does all things well.

Death meant gain for Paul in a number of ways. He was certain that when he left this earth he would actually be **'with Christ'** (1:23). Although he experienced something of the presence of Christ while he was on earth, in heaven he would actually be with his Lord and see him face to face (1 Cor. 13:12). Death would also be gain for Paul because it would open up the gateway to a much clearer knowledge and more joyful rejoicing than he had ever experienced on earth.[5]

Another reason why Paul looked forward to heaven was because he was ready to depart from this life. He says, **'I desire to depart and be with Christ, which is better by far'** (1:23). Paul always counted it a privilege to be able to suffer for his Lord. He urged Timothy, 'Do not be ashamed to testify about our Lord, or ashamed of me his prisoner. But join with me in suffering for the gospel, by the power of God, who has saved us and called us to a holy life' (2 Tim. 1:8-9).

He did not tell the Philippians about his dilemma because he wanted to escape the trials and problems of this life, but he looked forward to a day when he would be in infinitely closer fellowship with Christ. He had earlier written to the Corinthian church about this: 'If the earthly tent we live in is destroyed, [then] we have a building from God, an eternal house in heaven, not built by human hands' (2 Cor. 5:1). When he knew that he was approaching the end of his life, he was to tell Timothy that he was ready to depart (2 Tim. 4:6). He also says in his epistle to the Romans that we 'groan inwardly as we wait eagerly for our adoption as sons, the redemption of our bodies' (Rom. 8:18-23).[6]

Yet until the time of his departure he wanted to live for Christ (1:21). He was not selfish. His critics only wanted glory for themselves (1:15,17), but Paul only wanted Christ to be exalted in his body. His desire was that the Lord should be uplifted through his life for ever. This was an urgent matter for the apostle. He said that he desired this **'now as always'** (1:20).

If the Lord wanted him to carry on living and to be set free from his imprisonment, then he knew that this would result in **'fruitful labour'** for him (1:22). He would be free to travel once more to meet the believers in the various churches. He would be able to encourage them and teach them more about the Lord. He would also be free to visit places where the gospel had not yet been preached and have the opportunity to establish yet more companies of the Lord's people.

Although he would love to leave behind all the heartache and weariness of this life, Paul knew that it was **'more necessary'** for the Philippian believers that he should **'remain'** alive

(1:24). His concern was to be helpful to them and to be available to answer their questions. He longed to see their **'progress ... in the faith'** (1:25). This word 'progress' is the same one which is translated 'advance' in 1:12. The desire that was uppermost in Paul's mind was not that the congregation should increase in size, but that the believers should make progress in the Christian faith. He longed to know that they were increasing in the knowledge and love of God.

He also wanted to see their **'joy in the faith'** (1:25). He knew that Christians do not have to be miserable all the time. The most joyful people ought to be those who know and love the Lord. As they go about their daily lives, other people should be able to see by the way they conduct themselves that they have the joy and contentment of the Lord sustaining them — despite their circumstances (see 1:27).

As a believer faces death, his non-Christian friends should be able to tell that there is an assurance about him which shines out because he knows, for certain, that when he dies he is going to depart and go straight to be with Christ, which is better by far.

## Paul's choice

The apostle made no choice in the matter; he was content to leave it all in God's hands. This is why he said, 'For to me, to live is Christ and to die is gain.'

If these words, 'For to me, to live is...' were written out on a piece of paper and you were asked to complete the phrase, how would you fill it in? So many people would write, 'For to me, to live is to win several million pounds on the National Lottery,' or, 'For to me, to live is to be really famous and appear on all the top television shows.' Or would you write,

'For to me, to live is to get to the top of my profession and have a very powerful position with everybody running at my beck and call'?

Having completed the first part, how would you go on fill in the final part? What would you put for '... and to die is ...'? If, for you, living was winning several million pounds on the National Lottery, what would dying mean? It could only mean that you would leave it all behind. Or if, for you, living was being famous, what would dying mean? It might mean a lavish funeral attended by very famous people who made exuberant speeches saying what a wonderful person you had been. But what would happen to your fame? Certainly it would be preserved on film, videotape and in printed material, but what would it mean for you, lying in your coffin — dead? Finally, if for you, living meant being powerful, what would dying mean? It would only mean a few lines in the history books — and someone else taking your place at the office.

As Paul says in his letter to Timothy, 'We brought nothing into the world, and we can take nothing out of it' (1 Tim. 6:7). We all have to ask ourselves what living really means for us. Paul goes on to tell the Philippians, 'Whatever happens, conduct yourselves in a manner worthy of the gospel of Christ' (1:27). He also says, later in the letter, 'Whatever was to my profit I now consider loss for the sake of Christ. What is more, I consider everything a loss compared to the surpassing greatness of knowing Christ Jesus my Lord, for whose sake I have lost all things. I consider them rubbish, that I may gain Christ and be found in him, not having a righteousness of my own that comes from the law, but that which is through faith in Christ' (3:7-9).

# 6.
# Live worthily

*Please read Philippians 1:27-30*

Try to imagine yourself in the role of a mum or dad living in the 1920s, before our modern means of communication were readily available to everyone. You are standing on platform 8 of Victoria railway station, and your seventeen-year-old daughter is leaning out of a train window. The whistle blows and you know that any minute your little girl will be leaving you to go on a long journey hundreds of miles away to a foreign country. You are naturally very anxious about her because you know very little about the people she is going to work for. They have no phone and your only means of communicating with your daughter is going to be by letters, which will take many days to reach her. What are your parting words going to be as the train starts to move away? I suspect they will be something like, 'Goodbye, darling. Look after yourself, and whatever happens...' Well, what would you say? 'Whatever happens...' — what? In other words, what one thing would you want her to do, or refrain from doing, while she was in that far-off land?

Paul was in a similar situation. He was writing what might prove to be his final communication to his friends at Philippi. He knew that it was possible that he would soon be taken outside the prison and be executed. On the other hand, he might be set free and allowed to visit them once again.

So what message does he give the believers at Philippi? He tells them, **'Whatever happens** [whether I live or die], **conduct yourselves in a manner worthy of the gospel of Christ'** (1:27).


### They were to live for Christ

If they heard that Paul had been set free and was on his way to come and see them again, in what state would they want him to find them? Paul's dearest wish was to find them living **'in a manner worthy of the gospel'** (1:27), and they respected the apostle so much that they would not want to disappoint him. However, he did not want them to live worthily of the gospel just because he might arrive among them soon. His concern was that they were to live in such a way that they would not be ashamed of what they were doing, whoever came to see them. They were always to live their lives according to the gospel of Christ. They were to realize that, even if Paul could not see the kind of life they were living, Christ could.

The Lord has eyes which are as keen and penetrating as blazing fire (Rev. 1:14) and when he looks at any one of us, he not only sees us on the outside; he looks deep into our souls. His eyes search right inside our minds. He can see, not only what we do and say, but what we are thinking, and he can even see the motives which lie behind our actions.

But what if they never saw Paul again? He still wanted them to conduct themselves in a manner worthy of the gospel. Whatever else he heard about them, he wanted to hear that they were living their lives for the glory of God.

The word **'gospel'** comes twice in verse 27. This little word sums up the whole purpose of Paul's ministry. He wanted everyone to know the truth of the good news that God sent his only Son into this world to save sinners. His concern was also that this gospel message should not be compromised in any way by the lifestyle of the Philippian Christians.

We too should constantly be examining the way we live our lives to see if we are honouring the Lord and living in a manner that is worthy of the gospel of Christ.

Whatever happened to Paul or his readers, he wanted to hear that the Philippians were living as they should; in other words, he wanted them to remember their true citizenship. We noticed when we were looking at verse 1 that, although these believers were citizens of Philippi, they were also citizens of Rome. In 3:20 the apostle will go on to remind them that their citizenship is in heaven. This means that, just as they were always to behave in a way which upheld the laws and privileges of the city of Rome, so they must remember that, as Christians, they were also citizens of heaven. In other words, not only should they live by the principles of Roman rule, but by the values of the kingdom of God.

Whatever happened to them, Paul longed that they should remain faithful to the gospel. He might never see them again, but they still had a duty to be true to God's Word. Even if they too should be badly treated, each one of them must live in a way which honoured the gospel. Whatever happened to them as a result of the evil work of their enemies, they were to make sure that they stood firm in the things of the gospel.

Neither Paul nor they knew what trouble might come upon them as a result of Satan's activities, yet they were still to live in a manner worthy of Christ. How were they going to cope against the might of the Evil One? Warren Wiersbe maintains that 'The [most] important weapon against the enemy is not a stirring sermon or a powerful book; it is the consistent life of the believer.'[1]

**They were to be united**

This was the thrust of Paul's message to them: they were to stand firm in the faith, regardless of any opposition. There were people at Philippi who opposed the believers in their attempts to live for God (1:28). We do not know who these opponents were, but in 3:2 Paul tells his readers to 'Watch out for those dogs, those men who do evil, those mutilators of the flesh.' The Philippian believers would have known who these people were that Paul was writing about and, whatever happened, they were not to let themselves be intimidated by them.

Satan is always seeking to lead God's people astray. This is why Paul warns the Philippians to have nothing to do with these evil people. Instead they must conduct themselves in a manner worthy of the gospel of Christ. They were to live worthily by standing firm. They were to let nothing stop them from living for Christ. It takes great tenacity to stand firm against all opposition, but the Lord gives the necessary courage to those who are firm in their resolve to live their lives for his glory.

In the 1930s he gave great boldness to the 'small woman' Gladys Aylward, as she toiled hard leading hundreds of children to safety over treacherous Chinese mountains as she and her companions fled before the advancing Japanese army. He gave strength to Corrie Ten Boom as she sought to maintain her Christian faith in the Nazi Ravensbrook concentration camp. He still gives the determination to his faithful people to live for him despite all the pressures which come upon them in their daily lives.

The Philippians were to allow nothing to move them away from the faith which they had in Christ. This desire to remain firm in the faith is seen all through Scripture. Paul wrote to the Colossians, urging them to continue in their faith, 'established and firm, not moved from the hope held out in the gospel' (Col.

1:23). He also told the Corinthians to let nothing move them: 'Always give yourselves fully to the work of the Lord, because you know that your labour in the Lord is not in vain' (1 Cor. 15:58).

However, we shall never stand firm for the Lord unless we work hard at it. We shall never be strong believers if we just drift through the Christian life. Paul told the Ephesians that they should grow up and make sure that they were not 'tossed back and forth by the waves, and blown here and there by every wind of teaching' (Eph. 4:14).

The picture here is of an army who all **'stand firm in one spirit, contending as one man for the faith of the gospel'** (1:27). The gospel itself is under attack today. Even those who claim to be leaders of churches are watering down the truth of God's Word. They are saying things such as, 'Modern man has more insight that Jesus had; hell is just a state of non-being.'[2] In the face of this kind of teaching, Paul's call to stand together is addressed not only to the Philippian Christians of the first century A.D., but also to us, in our day, to march shoulder to shoulder to battle as we contend for the gospel of salvation.

If we are going to be united against the enemies of the gospel, then we must study the Bible together, we must pray together and we must work together. An efficient army trains together and this is why Paul urges the Philippians to 'stand firm in one spirit, contending as one man for the faith of the gospel'. Later in the letter he goes on to urge two ladies in the church at Philippi to 'agree with each other in the Lord' (4:2).

## They were not to be frightened

I imagine that there were many ways in which the opponents of the gospel tried to undermine the faith of the Philippian Christians. Sometimes they may have pretended to be very friendly towards them. Satan himself, although he is the prince of darkness, on occasions masquerades as an angel of light (2 Cor. 11:14). It is not surprising, then, that his agents also appear, at first sight, to be true teachers of God's Word. However, in fact, they are only misquoting and misapplying the Bible, with the sole intention of luring true Christians away from the gospel and to their ruin.

Because Satan works in this way we must always be on the alert. If we hear someone who is teaching something which is not in line with the Word of God, then we must beware of that person, even if he or she has a divinity degree, or holds high office in the church. That person may well be an enemy of the true gospel. We should test everyone who teaches us Christian things. Luke commended those of Berea who did not just accept what Paul said, but searched the Scriptures to see if he was telling them the truth (Acts 17:11). We too should study the Scriptures regularly to see that what we are being taught is the pure gospel.

We must also be on our guard because sometimes, instead of pretending to be friendly, Satan tries to frighten us into doing what he wants. Peter tells the believers of northern Turkey that the devil 'prowls around like a roaring lion looking for someone to devour' (1 Peter 5:8) and warns them to 'Resist him, standing firm in the faith' (1 Peter 5:9). So Paul tells the Philippians to contend as one man for the faith of the gospel, **'without being frightened in any way by those who oppose you'** (1:28). It is natural to be afraid of those who are more powerful than we are. But we must not be frightened in any way — provided, of course, that we ourselves are being true to the gospel.

*Why they were not to be afraid*

The Philippians were not to be frightened because *they were contending for the faith of the gospel.* They were men and women who had been called by the Lord into his service. This phrase, 'without being frightened in any way', was one which was used in classical Greek literature.

When I was very young my mother used to visit my granny in High Brooms, Tunbridge Wells. I cannot remember much about the old house where she lived, except that it had an outside toilet. But one picture, which hung on the wall of the living room, used to fascinate and frighten me. It was an old engraving of a battle-scene depicting men engaged in hand-to-hand combat. But what grabbed my attention was the left-hand corner of the picture. That whole corner was taken up by the face of a horse which had been wounded and brought down in the conflict. I can still see the bulging eyes of that poor beast — they were filled with terror.

That is the kind of picture which Paul's words might have conjured up in the minds of the Philippians. Anyone living in first-century Europe would have known that the noise of battle was so terrifying for the horses that they naturally turned their heads away in fear and tried to shy away from the fighting.[3] Paul was in effect saying to the Philippians, 'You must not be like frightened horses in battle. In fact, you are not to be frightened in any way. You must remember that the Lord Jesus Christ is the captain of your salvation and he is leading you onward to war against sin, Satan and this world.'

Another thing which would encourage them amidst the attacks of their enemies was the knowledge that *they were not alone in the battle*. Many others, throughout the world, were also contending for the faith of the gospel. Some were in prison because of their preaching, and yet others had been put to death for their faith. The Philippians were to take courage from this fact. This is why Paul reminded them of the time when he and Silas had been thrust into the inner prison at Philippi because they kept on preaching the good news about Jesus and the resurrection.

He writes, **'You are going through the same struggle you saw I had, and now hear that I still have'** (1:30). In other words he is telling them, 'Come on, brothers and sisters! We are all in this battle together.' This is the reason why he continually stresses the unity of those who are in Christ. We suffer with Christ — together. We stand firm in one spirit — together. We contend for the faith of the gospel — together. And we believe in him — together.

Finally, they were not to be frightened in any way because *they were suffering as Christians*. Peter tells his readers, 'Do not be surprised at the painful trial you are suffering... But rejoice that you participate in the sufferings of Christ, so that you may be overjoyed when his glory is revealed' (1 Peter 4:12-13).

### They were to rely on God's sign

The opposition which the Philippians were receiving was **'a sign'** from God (1:28). First of all, it was a sign *to those who oppose the gospel*. It was a sign that all those who are disobedient to the gospel message are on the wrong road. They are heading away from heaven. Indeed, everyone who turns his or her back upon Christ and his salvation is on that broad way which leads to hell (Matt. 7:13).

On the other hand, this opposition was also a sign *to those who were being persecuted for righteousness' sake* (Matt. 5:10). All of those who are true to God's Word, and are suffering for it, are on the way to heaven. Because they are suffering for Christ's sake, it is a sign that they will be saved.

Paul goes on to point out that both the destruction of the wicked and the salvation of the believers will be brought about **'by God'** himself (1:28). He is the one who will judge all things, and what he says cannot be contested by anyone. God has already fixed the day when he will judge the world. Paul tells us elsewhere that God 'has set a day when he will judge the world with justice by the man he has appointed' (Acts 17:31).

# 7.
# How to please your pastor

*Please read Philippians 2:1-4*

Paul was imprisoned in far-off Rome and he was not sure whether he was going to be released or executed. But one of the things which lifted his spirits was the thought of his dear friends at Philippi. They were a very loving group of people, and Paul rejoiced whenever he remembered them and prayed for them (1:3-4).

In what we know as his second chapter (of, course, he wrote it all as one letter, without any chapter breaks), he says in effect, 'Knowing that you are there, and that you are praying for me makes me glad; but do you know what would really cause me to be overjoyed? It would complete my joy if I learned that you had put all of your petty bickering behind you.' Or we can put what the apostle is saying to them like this: 'Where is your faith in Christ? He has called you to follow him. Why don't you live as he wants you to do?'

## Benefit from your faith

Faith is not a commodity that we are to keep shut up in a book. It is something which ought to work. It is not really faith at all if it does not display itself in some way. James says, 'Faith without deeds is dead' (James 2:26). He does not mean that we can only become Christians if we perform a certain amount of religious activities. On the contrary, what he means is: 'If you say you have faith in God, and that faith does not show itself in some way, then it is doubtful whether it is genuine faith at all.'

True faith in God is something which is very precious (2 Peter 1:1). It is something which is held in our *heads*. There are certain key doctrines of the Christian faith which we must believe if we are going to have genuine faith in God. We must believe that he is the Creator of all things, and that he made all things good. We must recognize that man, through his sin, has marred the beauty of God's world. And we must believe that 'God so loved the world that he gave his one and only Son, that whoever believes in him shall not perish but have eternal life' (John 3:16).

But not only is true faith something which we hold in our heads, it must be embraced in our *hearts* as well. We must accept that when Jesus died on the cross, he died to take away sin. However, before anyone can be cleansed from the guilt and power of his sins, he has to confess that he is a sinner, and that he is in the hands of God, who is angry at sin — so much so that he cannot even look upon anything which is impure.

The only people who can bring joy to their pastor's heart are those who have true faith in God and who allow that faith to shine out in their lives. Faith is something which brings us great blessing.

First of all, Paul refers to the blessing of **'encouragement'**. He says that this encouragement comes from **'being united with Christ'** (2:1). If we are in Christ, if we are really bound up together with him — then whatever happens to us, we shall be safe for evermore. Such a condition will be a great encouragement to all who draw near to God in faith. They will be so excited about it that they will want to tell everyone else about it.

Secondly, there is the blessing of **'love'**. As the word 'his' is not in the original, no one is quite sure whether the apostle is writing about his own love for the Philippians, or their love for each other, but, whatever the case, it is God's love for his people which brings believers much **'comfort'** (2:1).[1]

If anyone has true faith in God, then that faith will show itself, because the believer will receive such an abundance of God's love showered upon him that it will automatically overflow to those around him. Where can we see God's love for his people most clearly and most powerfully? It is in the gift of his Son, the Lord Jesus Christ, who died on the cross so that his people will have their sins washed away and they will be granted the gift of eternal life (Rom. 5:8; 8:38-39; 1 John 3:16; 4:9-10,16). [2] All these blessings are summed up by Paul in Galatians 2:20 when he writes, 'I live by faith in the Son of God, who loved me and gave himself for me' (Gal. 2:20).

Thirdly, there is the blessing of **'fellowship'**. One of my dictionaries defines fellowship as 'a society of people sharing mutual interests, activities, etc.'[3] This could be translated to mean that there is a spirit of fellowship between people who have similar concerns and interests. While this is true generally, Paul is specifically speaking here about **'fellowship with the Spirit'** (2:1). There is nothing frightening about this Spirit. Most commentators take this verse to refer to the work of God the Holy Spirit in encouraging fellowship between God's people; that is why they give the word 'Spirit' a capital 'S'.[4]

The fourth blessing which Paul reminds the Philippians about is **'tenderness and compassion'** (2:1). Each of these attributes can be seen supremely in the life and death of the Lord Jesus Christ. It is he who brings with him encouragement, comfort, fellowship, tenderness and compassion. If we are united with Christ, through faith in him, then we too will be showing these blessings in our lives, and others will receive the benefits of them.

Each of these four incentives to Christian living⁵ is introduced by the word 'if...' This is purely a grammatical figure
of speech; it is not placed there to cast any doubt upon the
statements which follow. If we substitute the word 'since' for
'if', then we shall arrive at the sense of what Paul is saying. It
is also significant that in the Greek text the first word in the
chapter is 'Therefore...' The reason Paul starts off in this way
is because what he says in these opening verses of chapter 2
flows out of what he has just been writing about in the previous
verses: 'Whatever happens, conduct yourselves in a manner
worthy of the gospel... [Since] you have encouragement from
being united with Christ...' (1:27; 2:1).

## Live out your faith

If Paul's **'joy'** was to be made **'complete'**, then the Philippians
had to live their lives in such a way that he, and everyone else,
could see that their faith was alive and working. He explains
how this is to be done both positively and negatively.

### *What they were to do*

One of the ways in which they could show their faith positively
was by **'being like-minded'** (2:2). This literally means that
they were to 'think the same things'. Paul did not want them
to act like robots, primed and controlled by their leaders;
rather, he wanted them to have a common purpose as their aim
in life. Our thinking always controls our actions. We cannot
hope to do the right thing if our thinking is twisted and going
in the wrong direction. Paul wanted each of the believers at
Philippi to think right things, and he wanted all of them to think
these things together. It would bring him tremendous joy if he
knew that they had unity of mind and spirit in the way they
went about the business of living.

If they were to think the same things, then they were to have **'the same love'** (2:2). Love in any church fellowship ought to be very rich. The new command which Jesus gave his disciples was that they should love one another (John 13:34). I know that we say that we love all other Christians, but we usually mean that in some vague kind of way. The procedure we should adopt in loving one another is the one which the Lord taught his disciples: '*As I have loved you,* so you must love one another.'

*What they were not to do*

Those are the positive aspects of what Paul wanted his readers to do. But there was also a negative way in which they could bring him great joy. They were to refrain from acting **'out of selfish ambition or vain conceit'** (2:3). Dr Martyn Lloyd-Jones was constantly telling preachers to watch the negatives and take very careful note of them. Those of us who have little children find that there are occasions when we have to call out to them, 'Don't do that!' That is what Paul is doing here when he says, **'Do nothing out of selfish ambition or vain conceit'** (2:3).

Paul means that they were not to behave as some of the Christians in Rome were doing. These people were preaching Christ, but they were doing so 'out of envy and rivalry ... out of selfish ambition, not sincerely, supposing that they can stir up trouble for [Paul]' (1:15,17). The apostle knew how easy it is for believers who are being successful in the work of the Lord to become puffed up with a pride in their own achievements. When preachers are patted on the back too often, they are tempted to feel good about their achievements — and this can so easily lead to pride. There is a great difference in a preacher being satisfied with a job well done and a pastor becoming conceited because he thinks that he has been very clever. It is right that ministers should have joy in their work for the Lord, and they should have a certain contentment in a job which has been done well, but all of us must constantly bear in mind that if we have done anything at all for the Lord it has only been achieved in God's strength, and the glory should go to him.

If we are true Christians, then God has graciously given us his great salvation and no one can take that away from us (John 10:28). The blessings of eternal life are all of his grace. These belong to us for all eternity, but the wonderful thing about God's grace is that it can grow. Indeed, it should grow, and we ought to become better and stronger Christians as a result of God's power flowing within us day by day.

However, God not only gives us his grace, he also gives us faith to trust in him for every need. The Scriptures also use the word 'faith' to describe the whole teaching of the Bible. This is sometimes called 'the faith'. We have been given this faith so that we can preserve it and make sure that nothing is allowed to corrupt it.

If we are to be people of faith, then we must have **'humility'** (2:3). The Scriptures constantly exhort us to be humble (e.g. Prov. 3:34; Matt. 23:12; James 4:6). Richard Halverson said, 'The greatest men are those who are humble before God. The tallest men are those who bend before God.'[6] We know little about the believers at Philippi, but surely Paul could not have prayed for them with joy had he not known that they were being effective in their Christian witness. Yet even in Philippi it seems that there were some who needed to be reminded to exercise more humility. This may be why Paul wrote, **'In humility consider others better than yourselves'** (2:3).

The apostle was writing this to all of the members of the church, not just to the overseers and deacons. He continues to stress this aspect of unity as he addresses himself to **'each of you'** (2:4). He is saying, in effect, 'I want each one of you to be humble.' He is telling all of them to be more humble than the most insignificant member of the church.

This emphasis on the need to be humble must have come a bit hard to many of these people who were Greeks, because heathen writers almost always used the word 'humility' in a bad sense, with the meaning of 'grovelling' or being 'abject'.[7] But Paul lifts this word up and gives it a Christlike character. A few verses later, he makes the following, truly staggering, statement: 'Christ Jesus ... humbled himself and became obedient to death — even death on a cross!' (2:5,8). Paul himself could also say to the Ephesian elders, 'I served the Lord with great humility and with tears' (Acts 20:19).

Secondly, Paul wanted the Philippians to put the interests of all the other believers before their own interests: **'Each of you should look not only to your own interests, but also to the interests of others'** (2:4). If they wanted to make Paul's joy overflow, then they should think of others much more than they thought of themselves. Christians are much too concerned about themselves and how things are going to affect them. Very many people come to church just to get something out of it for themselves. They forget that the needs of others — especially those who do not yet know the Lord as their Saviour — should be paramount.

What Paul said to the Philippians is so clear that it does not need any further explanation. People know if they are putting their own interests before the interests of others. If there is an element of this in the life of anyone reading this book then, before blessing can be received, it has to be rooted out.

How can we get rid of selfishness from inside of us? We can only do it by following Paul's instructions here because they are God's commandments to us. The apostle says, 'Your attitude should be the same as that of Christ Jesus' (2:5).

How could the Philippians complete Paul's joy? They could do it by living a much more Christlike life. How can church members today bring joy to their pastor's heart? They can do it by taking encouragement from being united with Christ, by taking comfort from his love, by enjoying fellowship with the Holy Spirit, by being tender and compassionate, by being united in mind, spirit and purpose and by showing humility towards others. All believers can encourage their leaders by considering that others are better than themselves. They can do it by turning away from what they want and elevating the interests of other people. And they can bring pleasure to their elders by letting their attitude to everything be the same as that of Christ Jesus, who humbled himself and obeyed his Father's will.

# 8.
# Imitate Jesus the Lord

*Please read Philippians 2:5-11*

Almost every time I see our oldest church member she says, 'Isn't the world in an awful mess?' She is blind and her only human companionship, for hours at a stretch, is provided by her radio. Apart from a few, mainly poor-quality, religious broadcasts, she listens to the news. However, it worries her that the radio appears to concentrate on all the bad things happening around the world, and it seldom gives reports of happy events.

The situation was similar in Paul's day. As he sat in his prison and thought about all the small groups of God's people, he must often have wondered what was happening to the world and how it was affecting the churches. When he listened to what his visitors told him, and as he read various letters which were sent to him, he must often have been cast down by the wrong attitudes displayed by so many people who ought to have known better. He heard about Christians who were discouraged and others who had found little comfort in their faith. But instead of such gloomy topics he longed to hear about greater love, fellowship, tenderness and compassion in the places outside his cell.

As he meditated upon these things, he wrote to the Philippians and urged them to be united in Christ. He wanted them to get rid of all thoughts of selfish ambition and vain conceit. He exhorted them to be humble and to have a greater concern about the needs of others than their own desires.

Having urged the Philippians to be humble, Paul instructed them to put the needs of others before their own. In doing so he tells them, **'Your attitude should be the same as that of Christ Jesus'** (2:5), or, as the Authorized Version puts it, 'Let this mind be in you, which was also in Christ Jesus.'

## Copy the servant mentality of Jesus

The greatest example which Paul could give them to imitate was the Lord Jesus Christ. He said, **'Christ Jesus ... being in very nature God, did not consider equality with God something to be grasped'** (2:5,6). Even though the Lord was so great and held such a high and holy position, he never thought that his divinity should be clutched hold of in a selfish way. A lesser man might well have used such privileges to promote himself, just as many candidates for political office seem to do; Jesus thought only of others and their needs. He did not assume that his equality with God was something to be exploited, or taken advantage of for his own ends. 'Unlike many oriental despots who regarded their position for their own advantage, Jesus understood that equality with God did not mean "getting" but "giving".'[1] He was in the form of God (indeed, he had always possessed the nature of God, he continued to have this while he was on earth and he is still endowed with deity now that he is back in glory). Yet at his incarnation he left heaven's glory and came to this earth to be among his people as 'one who serves' (Luke 22:27). He came to seek and to save the lost (Luke 19:10).

What did Paul mean by saying that Jesus is 'in the form of God'? (2:6, AV). The English word 'form' usually refers to the outward shape of an object; Paul uses it in that way when he speaks of those who have 'a form of godliness' but deny the power of it (2 Tim. 3:5). But we can also use the word in a much more comprehensive way. We can, for example, describe a cricketer as being 'on good form'. When we use that expression we mean much more than that his outward appearance is pleasing; we are referring to his whole person and the way this affects his actions. We mean that his mental, physical and emotional abilities are all working together in perfect harmony and are achieving the very best results possible.[2]

So when Paul speaks of Jesus being 'in the form of God', he certainly means to convey far more than the idea that he had the outward shape or likeness of God. Jesus did not merely give us an idea of what God is like. 'He is the image of the invisible God, the firstborn over all creation... He is before all things, and in him all things hold together' (Col. 1:15,17). 'The Son is the radiance of God's glory and the exact representation of his being, sustaining all things by his powerful word' (Heb. 1:3). John tells us that 'In the beginning was the Word, and the Word was with God, and the Word was God. He was with God in the beginning... The Word became flesh and made his dwelling among us' (John 1:1-2,14).

We now come to another question which has caused many to stumble and depart from sound doctrine: 'What did Paul mean when he wrote, **"[He] made himself nothing"** (or "He emptied himself")?' (2:7). Of what did Christ empty himself? Charles Wesley says he 'emptied himself of all but love'.[3] Many have concluded that the hymn-writer meant that when Christ came to this earth he gave up his divinity completely and all he retained was some vague ability to love; yet John tells us that 'God is love' (1 John 4:8,16), and the love of which God consists is so tremendous that it embraces every attribute of God.

Some have taught that 'At the incarnation Christ divested himself of the "relative" attributes of deity, omniscience, omnipresence and omnipotence, but retained the "essential attributes" of holiness, love and righteousness.'[4] However, there is no scriptural basis for any division of Christ's attributes.

O'Brien tells us that 'Christ emptied himself' is equivalent to Isaiah's statement that 'He ... poured out his soul unto death' (Isa. 53:12, AV). In other words, this expression used in Philippians 2:7 refers not to the incarnation, but to the surrender of Jesus' life upon the cross.[5]

So we see that any explanation of these words which diminishes Christ's divinity is erroneous. The fact is that Jesus was, and is, both God and man at the same time! His two natures remain distinct from each other, yet he is the God-man. If he was not God he would not have had the power to take away sin; and if he was not a perfect man his sacrifice for sin would not have been effective.

Yet, despite that indisputable fact, Christ took **'the very nature of a servant, being made in human likeness'** (2:7). Paul uses the same Greek word as in verse 6. This same Christ, who was in the form of God, was made 'in the form of a servant'. This does not mean that he exchanged the form of God for the form of a servant when he took flesh upon himself.[6] Christ became a servant in order to accomplish his mission of salvation.

It cannot be emphasized enough that Jesus was, and still is, God; yet he became a servant. But he was no ordinary man. Paul told the Romans that he is 'Christ, who is God over all' (Rom. 9:5). Even though the Lord underwent much deprivation and suffering, he never ceased to be divine. In his essential being he had the very nature of God. Not for one moment did he lay aside his Godhead, despite the attempts of the devil to divert him from his divinity; he still held the essential form of God (Col. 1:15; Heb. 1:3).[7]

*What becoming a servant meant for Christ*

Now let us look at some of the effects of Jesus' servanthood.

Firstly, in heaven he was free from the burden of sin, but when he came down to this earth he was surrounded by the filth of iniquity. He saw men and women blatantly rejecting the just laws of God as they turned their backs on so many things that God had commanded them to do. Yet the Lord made himself nothing, and one of the things that happened to him, as a consequence, was that he was tempted. Satan had no doubt that Jesus was God. Otherwise he would not have tempted him to turn the stones into bread, or throw himself off the highest point of the temple (Luke 4:1-13). Jesus never had to put up with that kind of testing in heaven, but for our sakes he made himself nothing and had to undergo such things.

Secondly, in heaven he enjoyed eternal bliss. In his high-priestly prayer he spoke of the glory he had with the Father before the world began (John 17:5). However, for a time, he turned his back upon all of that and made himself nothing. As Paul put it when writing to the Corinthian church, 'You know the grace of our Lord Jesus Christ, that though he was rich, yet for your sakes he became poor, so that you through his poverty might become rich' (2 Cor. 8:9).

And, thirdly, in heaven Jesus could exercise great authority, but when he came to this earth he made himself nothing and laid that power aside for a while. He told his hearers, 'By myself I can do nothing; I judge only as I hear, and my judgement is just, for I seek not to please myself but him who sent me' (John 5:30). He never gave up his authority while he was on earth, but he chose not to exercise it because 'Although he was a son, he learned obedience from what he suffered' (Heb. 5:8).

*Christ's servanthood as an example for us*

Bearing all of that in mind, the apostle says to the Philippians, **'Your attitude should be the same as that of Christ Jesus'** (2:5). He means that *none of us is to behave in a boastful way.* If we have risen to any height in society, or business, or the church, then we should remember that this is not something to boast about, as though we had achieved it through our own efforts alone. Jesus made himself nothing, and he voluntarily laid aside his heavenly glory. We too should acknowledge that if we have achieved anything at all in this life, then it is only by God's goodness and help that we have been able to rise to that position. That is not to deny that there is a sense in which it was our hard work which got us where we are today, but we must always acknowledge that the credit is due to God, for any abilities we possess, physical or intellectual, are themselves the gifts of God and it is only because he has given us these things, and the health and strength to avail ourselves of them, that we are able to do anything at all.

Jesus also showed *selfless devotion towards pleasing his Father*, and that should be our aim too. Jesus thought of others and spent his time and energy ministering to their needs. We too should seek to promote the interests of others, rather than our own welfare.

When Jesus came to this earth *he did not come to carry out his own will.* In the garden of Gethsemane he prayed, 'My Father, if it is possible, may this cup be taken from me. Yet not as I will, but as you will' (Matt. 26:39). We too are to have that same servant mentality. We should have the same attitude as that of Christ Jesus.

Jesus told his disciples, 'Now that I, your Lord and Teacher, have washed your feet, you also should wash one another's feet. I have set you an example that you should do as I have done for you' (John 13:14-15).

**Follow in the footsteps of Christ's humility**

Jesus was not ashamed to be **'found in appearance as a man'**
(2:8). He left all the glories of heaven and was made in human
likeness. At Bethlehem he underwent a natural, human birth.
He 'grew in wisdom and stature, and in favour with God and
men' (Luke 2:52). He learned a trade. He knew what it was to
be hungry and thirsty. He became weary at the end of the day
and he enjoyed the rejuvenating power of sleep. He suffered
real pain and anguish as he was nailed to the cross of Calvary.
In fact, he was made just like us and he shared in our humanity
as he was made like his brothers in every way (Heb. 2:14,17).

No one doubted that Jesus was a real man. When people
saw him they did not immediately fall down before him and
acknowledge that he was God. Instead they sometimes told
him to 'clear off'. They would not have treated him like that
if they had recognized his deity. As Jesus walked this earth, he
was immediately recognizable as a human being, because he
looked like a man. 'He wore the clothes and acted like the men
of his generation.'[8]

Not only did Jesus take on the appearance of a man, **'He
humbled himself and became obedient to death — even
death on a cross!'** (2:8). Paul says, 'He humbled himself.' It
was not that Jesus found himself trapped in such a way that he
could not escape, or that he was put to death against his will.
No, he humbled himself and 'became obedient to death'. He
knew what he was doing and he went all the way to the cross
in obedience to his Father's will. On that cross he took on
himself the punishment for the sins of his people.

It was no ordinary death he endured. He suffered death 'on
a cross'. Crucifixion was especially invented by the Romans
to be inflicted upon traitors. Those who died by crucifixion
died a thousand deaths, because it was so very painful, and
those who were executed in that way took a very long time to
die. The Romans wanted their subject people to see a man

hanging on a cross and take note that if they did not want to suffer the same fate, then they should obey everything that Roman law demanded of them.

However, for the Jews it meant something else, in addition to all of that. Anyone who died on a cross was under the curse of God (Deut. 21:23; Gal. 3:13). On the cross Jesus 'was forsaken by God and punished by him in body and in soul, experiencing the displeasure and damnation of God due to sinners'.[9] He was 'stricken by God' (Isa. 53:4). 'It was the Lord's will to crush him and cause him to suffer' (Isa. 53:10).

Imagine Paul, sitting in his prison cell, thinking about the Lord Jesus Christ and all he had done to save lost mankind. Paul would have realized that all the suffering he was going through in prison was nothing in comparison to what the Lord had been through for him. He would, therefore, have wanted his readers at Philippi to understand this. He wanted them to catch the same stupendous thought. He wanted them to rejoice that they were counted worthy to suffer disgrace for the name of Christ (see Acts 5:41).

We too should be willing to follow in Christ's footsteps. We cannot die to secure anyone's redemption, but we can have the same attitude of lowliness which Jesus displayed. We can humble ourselves and become obedient to our heavenly Father's will.

## Acknowledge his lordship

The humiliation and death of Jesus were not the end of the story. He did not remain in the grave. On the third day he rose up, triumphant over sin, death and the devil. He ascended up to the highest place in glory.

Paul wanted the Philippians to think deeply about these things. His concern was that they should meditate on the Lord. From the beginning of all things, Jesus was equal with God and reigned with him in heaven. At that time, and until he came to this earth, he was the highest of the high. But from that exalted position Jesus humbled himself and stooped down to the very lowest place on this earth. He was born of poor parents. He was laid in a manger because there was no room for them at the inn. He did not display his glories as he went around Galilee and Judea. He became, instead, a common servant. But not only was he among the lowest of the low, he suffered the death of a despised criminal. He underwent all of these things in order to pay the price of the sin committed by mankind. He did it all so that his redeemed people might go free. This is why Paul says, **'Therefore'** — it was because Jesus obeyed his Father's will and went to Calvary that **'God exalted him to the highest place'** (2:9).

*The name above every name*

It was the Lord God Almighty himself who lifted up Jesus and gave him the name that is above every name. Paul does not tell the Philippians at this point what that name is. He just says that the name is above every name. When we have children we often name them because we like the sound of a particular name, or because someone in the family has it. However, the names which we find in the Bible are all very significant. The name speaks of the person.

Two names are mentioned in these verses. There is the name **'Jesus'** (2:10), and we know that 'There is no other name [but the name of Jesus] under heaven given to men by which we must be saved' (Acts 4:12). The name Jesus is his human name, which refers to his work of redemption (such as we have in verses 7 and 8). But we also have in this passage the name **'Lord'**: **'Every tongue [shall] confess that Jesus Christ is Lord'** (2:11). This is his divine name.

*All will bow*

Paul now takes us from the depths in verse 8 to the heights in verses 9-11. He tells us that **'At the name of Jesus every knee should bow'** (2:10). He explains what he means by 'every'. He says that **'Every knee should bow, in heaven and on earth and under the earth'** (2:10). This has not yet happened. There has never been a time when everyone has bowed the knee to Jesus. So Paul must be talking about that great day towards which the whole of the Bible points and on which the whole world will be judged.

The apostle is obviously speaking about people here because things cannot bow the knee, neither do they have tongues. He is referring to all those who will be in heaven at that time when Christ comes again in great power and glory. He is also talking about those who will still be alive on earth at the time when he comes to judge the world. These include both those who own him as Lord and Saviour and those who refuse to accept his offer of salvation. Paul also speaks of those 'under the earth'. He must mean those poor demented souls in hell. There is no doubt in his mind that they will still be there on that day.

Every one of these people will bow to the Lord and every tongue will confess that Jesus is Lord. Isaiah prophesied about this time. He said that the Lord will say,

> Before me every knee will bow;
>     by me every tongue will swear.
> They will say of me, 'In the LORD
>     alone are righteousness and strength.'
> All who have raged against him
>     will come to him and be put to shame.
> But in the LORD all the descendants of Israel
>     will be found righteous and will exult
>
> (Isa. 45:23-25).

This is what is going to happen when the Lord comes again. Everyone will confess that Jesus Christ is Lord. Some will do it willingly because they know him as their Saviour and they love to confess his name. But others will do it unwillingly because they have denied the Lord of glory. However, even though they reject him now, on that great day they will confess him because they will have no alternative: the day of grace will have ended. In the very last chapter of the Bible we read, 'Let him who does wrong continue to do wrong; let him who is vile continue to be vile; let him who does right continue to do right; and let him who is holy continue to be holy' (Rev. 22:11). On that day there will no longer be any opportunity for repentance because the day of grace will have come to an end.

No one will be absent on that day. Every knee shall bow and every tongue will confess that Jesus Christ is Lord. Each one will say this, willingly or unwillingly. The question for all of us is: 'Will I confess the Lord willingly or unwillingly?'

# 9.
# Shine brightly

*Please read Philippians 2:12-18*

As Paul sat writing to the believers at Philippi, he must have wondered how he could encourage them to continue with their Christian endeavours. This was one of the reasons why he had directed their thoughts towards the Lord Jesus Christ. Because Christ was the sum and substance of their faith, then they should want to do something to express their obedience to his commands. The apostle desired that they should shine for the Lord. The way they could do that was by persevering in their faith, allowing nothing to dim their zeal for the gospel and bringing encouragement to others who were also seeking to shine for Jesus.

## Continue to shine

Paul rejoiced because the Philippians had obeyed the gospel when he had been with them. They had gone to all their friends and acquaintances and told them about the wonderful salvation that there is in Jesus for all who will turn to him in faith. They had not been shy in giving out this message of salvation. They were certain about what they believed and they were not slow to tell others about it. They not only spread the good news

about Jesus, but they urged those who heard their message to
obey the gospel.

The Philippians had obeyed the gospel themselves, but they
also pleaded with others to obey it. They knew that it was a
vital matter that everyone should respond to the call to repent
and believe the gospel. No Christian should have the attitude
which says, 'Oh well, I've told them about Jesus; now it's up
to them what they do about it.' Neither should we ever say to
ourselves, 'Well, salvation is of the Lord. I can't do anything
to save them. I'll just have to wait and see if God does anything
to stir them into spiritual life.'

Paul never behaved like that. He writes to the Thessalonians that '[God] will punish those who do not know God
and do not obey the gospel of our Lord Jesus' (2 Thess. 1:8).
He also tells the Corinthians, 'Knowing ... the terror of the
Lord, we persuade men' (2 Cor. 5:11, AV).

One of the reasons why the apostle wanted the Philippians
to continue to shine for Jesus was because he knew that this
would build them up in their own faith. So he tells them,
**'Continue to work out your salvation'** (2:12). The
Philippians would have understood that Paul did not mean by
this that any of their good deeds would save them from their
sins, or earn them good marks in God's book of merit. The
apostle had constantly taught that no one can earn his own
salvation. As he tells the Ephesians, 'It is by grace you have
been saved, through faith — and this not from yourselves, it is
the gift of God — not by works, so that no one can boast' (Eph.
2:8-9).

Salvation is a very large word. When we are 'born again'
(John 3:3), we are saved and have been called out of darkness
into God's wonderful light (1 Peter 2:9), but that is not all there
is to salvation. Writing to the Corinthians, Paul explains our
salvation in the past, the present and in the future. He writes,

'[God] has delivered us from such a deadly peril, and he will deliver us. On him we have set our hope that he will continue to deliver us' (2 Cor. 1:10). Here, in Philippians, the apostle means that 'Their salvation is a process (Luke 13:23; Acts 2:47; 2 Cor. 2:15). It is a process in which they themselves, far from remaining passive or dormant, take a very active part. It is a pursuit, a following after, a pressing on, a contest, fight, race.'[1]

So, although our good works cannot gain us salvation from sin, we are still required to do good. These good deeds are both an evidence of our salvation and a sign of our spiritual development. Peter tells us that we should 'grow in the grace and knowledge of our Lord and Saviour Jesus Christ' (2 Peter 3:18).

However, every action of the believers must be carried out in a right spirit. It is an awesome thing to declare the unsearchable riches of Christ (Eph. 3:8). So we should never treat the salvation which Christ has wrought in a flippant or light-hearted manner. On the contrary, we should seek to live lives which are glorifying to God **'with fear and trembling'** (2:12), not because God is a tyrant and we are afraid that he might change his mind and send us to hell after all, but because we have an awesome and highly respectful attitude towards our holy, gracious and blessed God.

When Paul told the Philippians to do this work with fear and trembling, he did not mean that they should be hesitant about it. They should spread the good news knowing, for certain, that God was working within them. We can be confident, too, that the Lord will ensure that our work of evangelism will be done in his strength. Paul had told the Philippians that he was confident that he (i.e. God) who had begun a good work in them would carry it on to completion (1:6). Therefore, as the work of salvation was God's, God would give the power and the ability needed to perform this work. After all, it is his good purpose that as many as possible should hear the message of salvation and obey it.

## Let nothing dim your light

There are many things which can diminish our enthusiasm for Christian work.

### *Hindrances from within the fellowship*

Paul first of all mentions those within the fellowship of God's people who put stumbling-blocks in the way of those who are seeking to spread God's Word. These are the people who are constantly complaining about all manner of things.

When I was the manager of a shop selling books and stationery, it was those customers who continually found fault with things who made my work difficult. People like that are found in all walks of life and in all kinds of situations. Unfortunately they are also found within the membership of churches. The pastor who has in his congregation people who regularly find fault over petty matters is made to wonder whether his work is worthwhile. It is such people who sometimes drive pastors to resign from their churches.

Paul urged the Philippians not to have that kind of attitude. Instead they were to **'Do everything without complaining'** (2:14). Those who complain in the sense which Paul means here are being selfish (see Matt. 20:11). They are being critical about very small points. They are acting like the Pharisees and the teachers of the law who complained to the disciples of Jesus, 'Why do you eat and drink with tax collectors and sinners?' (Luke 5:30).

Sometimes when people complain there is some matter which needs to be examined and put right, but they raise it in the wrong spirit. An example of this in Scripture is the case of those who complained that certain 'widows were being overlooked in the daily distribution of food' (Acts 6:1). It was correct that they should point out an injustice, but they did so in a complaining way rather than making a constructive suggestion.

Paul also said that if we do not want our light to be dimmed, then we should avoid **'arguing'** (2:12). 'Complaining and arguing' describe exactly what the children of Israel did in the desert.² They grumbled against Moses when they could not drink the bitter water of Marah (Exod. 15:24). They also complained frequently against Moses and Aaron in the course of their wanderings in the desert. Eventually Moses told them that their complaints were not really directed against him and his brother, but against the Lord himself (Exod. 16:8).

### The world outside

However, it is not only a wrong spirit within the fellowship which causes the light of the gospel to be dimmed; the state of the world around us also has a dampening effect upon the work of God. The apostle reminds the Philippians that they were living among **'a crooked and depraved generation'** (2:15).

It is still the same today. All around us is darkness. In a physical sense there are many places where there is plenty of bright light, and where flashing colour strobes pick out the gyrating bodies of young people dancing to very loud music. But Paul had a word to describe all 'excitement' of that kind: he called it 'darkness'. He said that this world needs the light of the gospel to shine out into it and dispel the spirit of the age.

When he spoke of 'this ... crooked generation', he meant
that the people were all bitter and twisted inside. They were off
course and heading away from God. All those, in every age,
who do not know the light of the gospel shining in their hearts
are crooked inside and heading towards a Christless eternity.

Paul also describes the world as 'depraved'. This word has
more to do with the outward behaviour of the people of the
world. Without a knowledge of Christ and his salvation, there
is no hope for anyone.

In view of the state of the world, Christians can only **'shine
like stars in the universe'** (2:15; cf. Rev. 21:11) if they remain
uncontaminated by it. This is why Paul says that God's people
must live in a way which is **'blameless and pure'** . He wants
us *all* to be wholesome. We must be like a piece of metal which
has no impurities in it, or like wine or milk which has not been
diluted. We must be on the inside what we appear to be on the
outside. In other words, we must be free from the contamination of this world. William Barclay says, 'The Christian life
must be such that it can be offered like an unblemished
sacrifice to God.'[3]

We are to remember that we are **'children of God'** (2:15).
That means that we should delight in obeying our heavenly
Father. We should want to do what pleases him. Therefore, we
should do everything in our power to live **'without fault'**. We
should remember that he wants us to be holy, because he is
holy (1 Peter 1:16). We shall only be able to shine brightly for
God if we allow nothing to dim our light. One of our major
tasks as believers is to **'hold out the word of life'** (2:16). Jesus
said that we should let our light shine before men, that they
may see our good deeds and praise our Father in heaven (Matt.
5:16).

Just as stars dispel physical darkness when they shine out
brightly on a clear, cold, frosty night, so our lives are to shine
out with the light of God's salvation to banish spiritual and

moral darkness from the world. The light which we are required to hold out is not our own light; it is God's light. However, we are to be like a lighthouse shining out into the darkness of this world with the truth of God.[4]

## Bring encouragement to other believers

No sensible person pretends that being a Christian is easy. Paul had put a great deal of effort into building up new Christians in the faith. He now uses one of his favourite phrases and calls the Christian life a race (cf. Acts 20:24; 1 Cor. 9:24; Gal. 2:2; 5:7; 2 Tim. 4:7-8). The apostle also knew that it required a great deal of hard work to build churches for God's glory and he was aware that working on the land required much strenuous effort if a harvest was going to be gathered one day (see 2 Tim. 2:6).

When he remembered the Philippians, and other believers, Paul felt that he had something to be proud of. He was not thinking of boasting in a selfish way. He meant that he could be satisfied with a job which had been well done. That is why he said, 'If I am to be executed now, then I am ready,' or, to quote his own words, **'If I am being poured out like a drink offering on the sacrifice and service coming from your faith, I am glad and rejoice with all of you'** (2:17). The thought of sacrifice took Paul's mind back to the regulations in Numbers 15:3-10, where we learn that drink libations were offered along with other sacrifices. Together they made an aroma pleasing to the Lord. Paul had been urging these Philippian believers to live sacrificial lives; now he is saying that he is ready, if necessary, to offer his own life as a drink offering, and his sacrifice would mingle with theirs and be acceptable to the Lord. He also trusted that his readers would be glad and would rejoice with him.

He knew that, ultimately, it is not our comfort in life which matters most. It is our obedience to God which brings deep, lasting satisfaction to us. It also brings encouragement to others who labour for the spread of the gospel light amid the darkness of this universe. John describes how the gospel glorifies God in this way: 'In [Christ] was life, and that life was the light of men. The light shines in the darkness' (John 1:4-5). The same God 'who said, "Let light shine out of darkness," made his light shine in our hearts to give us the light of the knowledge of the glory of God in the face of Christ' (2 Cor. 4:6).

# 10.
# Serve faithfully

*Please read Philippians 2:19-24*

Those who read through Philippians carefully from beginning to end will certainly be brought up sharp when they reach chapter 2:19. At first sight it may seem as if Paul has lost his train of thought, or is digressing. He has been talking about a number of great doctrinal subjects. He has written about the Lord Jesus Christ and who he is, and he has given his readers instructions on their need to live holy lives. Then, suddenly, he starts to discuss certain domestic arrangements which he is in the process of making.

Of course, those who attempt to prove that this is a letter of merely human origin, and not divinely inspired, will say that these verses are not part of the original letter, or that they really belong at the end of the epistle. They believe that such mundane matters would not have interrupted Paul's teaching. However, those who believe that the Scriptures are without error will find that difficult to believe. They will affirm that this section is placed at this point because Paul wanted to talk about his good friends Timothy and Epaphroditus in this part of his letter. These verses are not a distraction from the main teaching of the letter at all. They are 'a practical manifestation and demonstration of what the apostle had already been laying down'.[1]

## Paul's desire

Although he was in prison and suffering great hardship, the
apostle was not preoccupied with his own discomfort. His
burning concern was for the welfare of the believers at
Philippi. He was not feeling miserable because of the way he
was being treated; he was anxious to discover how the
Philippians were coping with the pressures of life as Christians. He knew that, wherever the gospel had been preached
and people had come to know the Lord as their Saviour, there
the devil was active.

Even in Rome many believers in Christ only thought of
themselves and their own interests. They made sure that they
took first place in everything. They did not consider that the
needs of other Christians were more important than their own,
and they certainly did not have much time for the well-being
of those who were completely outside of Christ. A friend wrote
me a letter in which she said, 'One proof of our love for God
is our love for our neighbour.'[2] We can see that many of the
people around Paul were not manifesting such love because he
says, **'Everyone looks out for his own interests, not those of
Jesus Christ'** (2:21).

These church members were acting just as they had in the
days before they had come to know Christ as their Saviour.
Paul had admonished the believers at Corinth some years
earlier with the words: 'You are still worldly. For since there
is jealousy and quarrelling among you, are you not worldly?
Are you not acting like mere men?' (1 Cor. 3:3-4). It was
impossible for those who were looking out for their own
interests to have the same attitude as Christ when he made
himself nothing and took the very nature of a servant (2:7). So,
when non-Christians saw how these church members conducted themselves they may well have said to each other,
'These people are no better now than they were before they

believed in Jesus Christ.' That was the state of things among the Christians at Rome.

However, Paul knew that it was not only the believers at Rome who were behaving like that. In other places too Christians were behaving selfishly (see 2:3). Even among the church at Philippi, who in many ways were a source of such joy to the apostle, there were some who caused tension in the fellowship of God's people (4:2). That may have been one of the reasons why Paul wanted to send someone to them — in order to help resolve the tensions in their fellowship.[3]

Sadly, there are Christians today who are behaving in this same self-centred way. In the personal letter that I quoted earlier my friend also said, 'Satan is working overtime now. You see him in churches today. There is more commotion and emotion than devotion.'

As Paul thought about the condition of the churches, he was cast down. He feared that Satan was getting the upper hand at Philippi and he could hardly wait to learn that his fears were groundless. Although the apostle had a very firm trust in God, he was also very human. We can tell that because he writes of his anxiety to hear how things were going with the believers at Philippi (see 2:28).[4]

There was one thing which would cheer him up, and that would be to learn some good news about his friends. The preaching of the gospel of salvation had brought all of them great joy. As we saw earlier, Paul had been present when many of them had received the Lord as their Saviour and now he wanted to hear further good news of them. He longed to know that they were progressing in the Christian faith and that they were continuing to work out their salvation with fear and trembling (2:12). He sought assurances that they were constantly active in holding out the word of life in the darkness that was all around them. Each one of these things would have brought him great joy (2:18).

Therefore, to find out how they were coping in their Christian lives, Paul planned to send Timothy and Epaphroditus to them. He was looking forward to the day when he, himself, could come and visit them, but until then he would send two of his fellow-workers to see them. He was particularly keen that Timothy should accompany Epaphroditus when the latter returned home, because Timothy could bring back to the apostle news of how things were going at Philippi.

As the court had not yet given its verdict, Paul did not know whether he would be executed or released, but he was not anxious about himself. However, his hope was not in Nero, to whom he had appealed. He knew that his future did not depend upon a mere man — even one as powerful as the Roman Emperor. His hope was in the Lord. In fact, the whole of his life was dominated by the Lord Jesus Christ. We can see that by the very way in which he tells the Philippians of his intention to send Timothy to them: **'I hope in the Lord Jesus to send Timothy to you soon'** (2:19). He writes in similar terms of his hope that he himself might be free to come and see them again: **'I am confident in the Lord that I myself will come soon'** (2:24).

### Timothy's task

The apostle's companion, Timothy (see 1:1), was the ideal person for him to send to them. He was a comparatively young man who was well fitted for the task because he took **'a genuine interest in [the] welfare'** of the Philippians (2:20). He had been one of Paul's companions on the missionary journey during which the church in Philippi was founded (Acts 16:1-3,11-40; 1 Thess. 2:2) and he had returned to the church several times since (Acts 19:21-22; 20:3-6; 2 Cor. 1:1). Ever since those days he had taken a keen interest in each one of the believers in that city. When Paul said that Timothy had taken a genuine interest in the welfare of the Philippians, he meant that Timothy did something to show his concern for them. He obviously prayed for them and encouraged them in their spiritual growth, and now he was keen to visit them again.

We might have thought that Paul would have sent someone else, because Timothy was very precious to the apostle and could have been a great comfort to him in his imprisonment. However, Paul explains the reason why he sent Timothy, rather than someone else: **'I have no one else like him, who takes a genuine interest in your welfare'** (2:20). We know from other passages that Paul had other faithful helpers while in Rome, such as Luke and Aristarchus, but it seems that of those who were available at this time, Timothy was the only one who was prepared to put the interests of others before his own and so was willing to go to Philippi on Paul's behalf.

The fact that Timothy took an interest in the welfare of the Philippians was not his only qualification for this task. He had **'proved himself ... in the work of the gospel'** (2:22). He was someone who was prepared to roll up his sleeves and get his hands dirty in the cause of Christ. Paul said that **'As a son with his father he has served with me in the work of the gospel'** (2:22). Timothy had often worked alongside of Paul. He knew what it was to work as a member of a team. He was not someone who only wanted to work if he could do everything his way. He and Paul had worked together just as though they were father and son. That means that they had mutual love and respect for each other. Paul probably called Timothy his son (see 1 Tim. 1:2; 2 Tim. 1:2) because he had led him faith in Christ.

Timothy was qualified for this task because he was a man who knew what it was to serve. When the apostle said, 'He has served with me in the work of the gospel,' the word translated 'served' was the same Greek word that would be used of a slave. Everyone in the Roman world knew that a slave was someone who was totally in submission to his master. He had no rights of his own. His whole life was entirely in the hands of his owner, and he had to do whatever he was called upon to do, without question or hesitation. Timothy, like Paul, had proved himself to be one who was totally in submission to Christ. Like the Lord Jesus Christ, he delighted to obey his Father's will (Ps. 40:8; Matt. 26:39; Rom. 7:22).

Timothy must have been very valuable to Paul, particularly as the apostle was shut up in prison. Yet Paul was prepared to make the sacrifice of parting with him. He was so eager to hear news of the church at Philippi that he was willing to let Timothy go. This was because Paul had the mind of Christ. He put the interests of others before his own, and he was prepared to part with Timothy because it was in the interests of the Philippians to have Timothy with them for a while. In the same way God, our heavenly Father, was prepared to part with his beloved Son, the Lord Jesus Christ, because he wanted us to be saved from the guilt and power of our sin.

But Timothy, too, had the mind of Christ. There is absolutely no evidence to suggest that Timothy hesitated to follow out Paul's instructions. He gladly obeyed the call of Paul and travelled to Philippi to please the apostle.


**Our calling**

We do not live in the Roman Empire. Probably most people reading this book are not in prison. Yet if we belong to the Lord then we serve a heavenly Master who calls us to be as obedient to his voice as Timothy was to Paul's words. Unlike those in the first century, or many in poorer countries of the world even today, our lives in the West are comparatively easy. None the less God still calls us to be his slaves. There are people all around us who are in deep need. We should not be so taken up with our own interests that we spare no thought or concern for our less fortunate brothers and sisters.

It is salutary to ask ourselves what interest we take in the welfare of others. We should all be concerned about those who are fellow members with us in our congregation. We should speak to them often and enquire about their well-being. We should visit them and invite them into our homes. We should also be concerned about our neighbours and realize that we have a responsibility to tell them about Jesus and his love for sinners. We should help them in any way we can, especially if they are elderly or infirm.

We should also be concerned about others who live further afield. The plight of refugees should be in our minds and we should support, by prayer, encouragement and giving, missionaries working in far-flung places. We should be willing to make sacrifices for the benefit of those who are less well-off than ourselves.

We are servants of Christ, so we should be willing to obey the commands of our Saviour. Some Christians are more concerned to stay in their comfortable homes, well-paid jobs and friendly churches than they are to go out into all the world and preach the gospel to every creature.

Paul and Timothy were bondservants of Christ. How willing are we to put the welfare of others before our own comfort and well-being? Can it be said of you, 'He, or she, served in the work of the gospel'? Or are you one, like the vast majority of Christians in Paul's day, who 'looks out for his own interests, not those of Jesus Christ'? (2:21).

# 11.
# Care passionately

*Please read Philippians 2:25-30*

In 1996 there was a Channel 4 television series called *Dream Island*. Each programme featured various English girls who had gone on holiday to the Greek island of Zakinthos and had fallen in love with local men. All of them had given up everything in England to marry their boyfriends and settle down to live with them on that small Greek island.

The series told about the problems they faced in going to live in a totally different culture. One particular difficulty that they all had in common concerned their mothers-in-law. They found it very hard to accept that, in modern Greek culture, the husband's mother runs the home. They did not take very readily to having their mothers-in-law make all the major decisions concerning their children. They particularly found it hard to accept that the eldest daughter always had to be named after the husband's mother.

Apart from their mothers-in-law, the girls all had one other thing in common: from time to time they were dreadfully homesick. Any of us who have been away from our homes and loved ones will know what that is like. Those who go away to university at the age of eighteen experience it; girls who marry men who live far away in a different culture know what homesickness is like — and so did the lovely character whom we meet in Philippians 2:25-30, Epaphroditus.

## Epaphroditus had been sent to Paul

The Philippians had heard that Paul was in prison and they wanted to help him as much as they could. It was impossible for all of them to visit the apostle, so they sent a representative from their congregation. He was not one of the elders or leaders. Neither was he a spare church member who had nothing special to do. He was a loving, hard-working brother who offered to go to see Paul on their behalf. He was their messenger and his name, Epaphroditus, means 'lovely'.¹ He was someone who had a loving concern for Paul's welfare and he went to Rome for two reasons. Firstly, he was the bearer of a gift from the church at Philippi (4:18), and secondly, he was to be Paul's servant and companion in his imprisonment.

Epaphroditus proved to be just what Paul needed to help him in his captivity. The apostle obviously grew very fond of him. We do not know whether they knew each other before this time, but when Paul writes this letter he speaks of Epaphroditus in terms of great affection. He calls him **'my brother'**. He was not ashamed of that relationship because he emphasizes '*my* brother'.

All Christians are brothers and sisters of one another. There may not be a blood relationship between them, but through Christ's atoning blood they are united into the brotherhood of God's people. Paul was certainly not ashamed to call Epaphroditus 'my brother'. But the most stupendous news of all is that our Lord Jesus Christ himself is not ashamed to call all true believers his brothers (Heb. 2:11). How sad it is, then, when those who are united together in Christ, by virtue of his precious shed blood, refuse to have fellowship with each other because of some minor disagreement over the interpretation of Scripture.

Secondly, Paul calls Epaphroditus **'my ... fellow-worker'**. The task of being a Christian is hard work.

Epaphroditus certainly knew what it was to work hard for Christ. Paul tells us that **'He almost died for the work of Christ'** (2:30). This man worked alongside of Paul. The apostle does not say, 'He worked *under* me.' He describes him as his 'fellow-worker'. This visitor from Philippi was not afraid to be identified with Paul, who was in prison. He would have had every reason to be fearful because anyone consorting with a man in prison and facing possible execution in the way that Epaphroditus was doing was putting himself in danger of becoming involved with the same charge.[2]

Thirdly, Paul calls him **'my ... fellow-soldier'**. If you talk to any old soldier, especially from the days of the First World War, he will tell you what it meant to be comrades in arms. There is a strong camaraderie about being thrown together in wartime. The people of the East End of London discovered that during the blitz of World War II. When Buckingham Palace was bombed, the then queen (now the Queen Mother) said, 'I can now visit those poor people whose homes have been bombed, and I can now hold my head up high, because the same has happened to me.'

Any Christian who wishes to serve the Lord faithfully is going to be aware of enemies around him. Satan is always active in trying to cause havoc among the people of God. He does this by making some of them feel discontented. Perhaps this is why Paul writes, 'Do everything without complaining or arguing' (2:14). He influences others to grow cold in their faith, and he sends false teachers among them. These are those who claim to be men of God, yet they treat the Bible as though it is a man-made book which can be followed or ignored, depending on what is being taught. However, Epaphroditus was not someone who was easily put off by the devil and all his works. Paul tells us that he was his 'fellow-soldier'.

Fourthly, Epaphroditus had been sent **'to take care of [Paul's] needs'**. We do not know exactly what that entailed, but we can be sure that he did whatever he could to help the apostle. He gladly humbled himself and became Paul's servant. He was an illustration of what Paul had been teaching in 2:3: 'Do nothing out of selfish ambition or vain conceit, but in humility consider others better than yourselves.'

## Epaphroditus fell ill

We do not know whether he became unwell while he was on the long journey from Philippi to Rome, or whether he caught some awful disease when he visited Paul in his prison. However it happened, Epaphroditus became ill, very ill indeed. Three times Paul mentions this in these few verses. He tells us that Epaphroditus **'was ill, and almost died'** (2:27). He repeats this, saying, **'He almost died for the work of Christ'** (2:30) and emphasizes the point further by adding the words **'risking his life...'** (2:30). The expression Paul uses here is a gambling term.[3] It is like saying that Epaphroditus 'staked everything on the turn of a dice'. He gambled his very life when he wore himself out for the sake of the gospel and exposed himself to all kinds of dangers in carrying out the work he had been sent to do.

All of us who are believers in the Lord Jesus Christ need to ask ourselves, 'Am I willing to go to such lengths in my service for the Lord?' There are many thrilling missionary stories about people who risked their lives in their Christian service — men and women who suffered great privation, illness and dangers, all for the sake of the Lord and his work. These should be an encouragement to all of us to be prepared to risk our lives too for the sake of Christ. Whenever we are embarrassed to tell our friends that we are followers of Christ, we should remember how Epaphroditus risked his very life for the cause of the gospel.

*Why did Paul not heal him?*

A question may arise in our minds over Epaphroditus' illness. If we know anything at all about Paul and the way in which he had been enabled by the power of God to work many mighty miracles, we will surely want to know why he did not heal Epaphroditus when he was so very ill. The apostle was certainly very distressed by his companion's illness. He told the Philippians that if Epaphroditus had died he would have had **'sorrow upon sorrow'** (2:27). Yet he apparently did nothing to heal him. Why was that?

The obvious answer is that although Paul was on occasions used by God to heal certain people in specific circumstances, this gift of healing was in the sovereign hands of God. Dr Martyn Lloyd-Jones used to say, 'The apostles never put up notices saying, "Healings will take place here next Friday at 8 o'clock."' Scripture teaches us that the gift of healing is under the lordship of the Holy Spirit.[4] The sick are not healed just because a certain preacher commands them to be healed. It is so cruel and erroneous to teach that the reason why some people are not miraculously healed is because they have no faith, or that if someone dies as a result of an illness it is because he or she is lacking in faith. It is evil even to suggest such a thing.

When one of these so-called evangelists advertises for people to come to his meetings and see miracles happen, this can be positively harmful to the gospel message. We can imagine the case of a non-Christian who has a serious illness and goes along to such a gathering, but comes away unhealed. What is that experience going to say to that person about Christ and his gospel? It will do untold damage. Healing cannot just be performed at the flick of a switch, or in answer to an evangelist's prayer or touch.

Paul could not heal Epaphroditus (much as he would have longed to do so) even though the sick man was near to death's door. Nor could he heal Timothy (1 Tim. 5:23), Trophimus (2 Tim. 4:20), or even himself (Gal. 4:13-14). But although Paul could not heal Epaphroditus, God could. Paul simply tells us, **'He was ill, and almost died. But God had mercy on him, and not on him only but also on me'** (2:27). It is God alone who brings healing. This is why we cry out to him in prayer. Sometimes he chooses to answer our prayers and bring healing to an individual, but on other occasions he chooses not to do so. He heals according to his own will and pleasure.

### Epaphroditus was sent back to Philippi

This brother was very useful to Paul, but the apostle says he thinks it **'necessary to send [him] back'** to Philippi (2:25). The first reason for this was because he was homesick. Paul tells the Philippians, **'He longs for all of you'** (2:26). This is a very natural experience for those who are away from home, especially if it is for the first time in their lives.

The second reason why Epaphroditus wanted to go back to Philippi was because the members of the church there had heard that he was ill. He wanted to return so that they could see for themselves that he had completely recovered from his illness. It had distressed him greatly when he learned that his friends had heard of his illness. He loved his home church so much that he did not want them to be worried about him. He was so upset that Paul said that he was **'distressed'** (2:26). The Greek word used here is the one which is used to describe the emotions of the Lord when he was in the garden of Gethsemane. Matthew tells us that when Jesus prayed to his Father, just before his arrest, his soul was overwhelmed with

sorrow and he was 'troubled' (Matt. 26:37-38). That word,
translated 'troubled' in that passage, is the one which is
rendered 'distressed' here. That is how Epaphroditus felt
when he knew that his friends were worried about him. It is not
surprising that he wanted to go back to them.

Paul was no doubt aware that some people at Philippi might
have thought, when they heard that Epaphroditus had returned, that he was afraid to remain in Rome. We can imagine
them saying, 'He couldn't take the rigours of life in the
capital.' But that was not how Paul saw it. He carefully worded
his letter: **'I think it is necessary to send back to you
Epaphroditus'** (2:25). It was Paul's own decision to return
him. That was not because Epaphroditus could not stand the
pace, but because the apostle wanted the Philippians to be
spared anxiety about their mutual friend (2:28).

It was for this reason that Paul requested the church to give
Epaphroditus a warm welcome: **'Welcome him in the Lord
with great joy, and honour men like him'** (2:29). Their
church member had proved himself to be a faithful servant of
Christ, as Paul himself was. Therefore, they were to welcome
him with great joy. There was no shame in his return, as there
had been when Mark had deserted Paul and Barnabas in
Pamphylia (Acts 15:38).

The Philippians were to use Epaphroditus as an example of
those who care passionately for the needs of the saints. They
were also to honour all who behaved as he did. This man had
almost died for the work of Christ and he had risked his life to
serve the Lord on behalf of the church at Philippi.

Paul was not complaining about the Philippians when he
said that Epaphroditus had risked his life **'to make up for the
help [they] could not give'** him (2:30). He did not mean that
they had refused to help him. All he is saying here is that they
were not physically able to help him — but Epaphroditus did
so on their behalf.

## Epaphroditus is an example to all Christians

Like his Lord, Epaphroditus was a servant. Jesus 'made himself nothing, taking the very nature of a servant … he humbled himself ' (2:7,8). Like his Lord, Epaphroditus suffered agony on behalf of his friends. Jesus was greatly troubled in the garden of Gethsemane (Matt. 26:37). And, like his Lord, his friends are bidden to welcome him with great joy.

But the Lord Jesus Christ did so much more than Epaphroditus, or any man. He suffered the agony of the cross of Calvary to pay the price of the sin of his people. 'God made him who had no sin to be sin for us, so that in him we might become the righteousness of God' (2 Cor. 5:21). The call goes out, not just to the members of the Philippian church of long ago — it reaches out to all who will listen today. The message is: 'To all who received him, to those who believed in his name, he gave the right to become children of God — children born not of natural descent, nor of human decision or a husband's will, but born of God' (John 1:12-13).

# 12.
# Beware of religion!

*Please read Philippians 3:1-3*

A lady, whom I knew vaguely, telephoned me to ask if I could visit her because she was distressed. She told me that she did not go to church on Sundays, but she always tried to take communion on Thursday mornings. By her own admission she was relying on her religious observances to ensure that she ended up in eternal bliss.

Some years before this a man who lived near me explained that he did not need to go to church because, as he said, 'I can be just as good a Christian, better in fact than many, by doing my best to help people.' That man was depending upon his good works for God to have mercy upon him when the time came for him to leave this life. And there are many other people who claim that they can worship God in the open air so well that they do not need to go to church services. They think that because they admire God's handiwork in nature he will look favourably upon them and save them at the end of their days.

But Paul was not writing to people who had ideas like that. He was writing to those who knew that they could not gain access to heaven merely because they said prayers, or attended church, or took part in religious ceremonies, or lived good lives, or respected God's creation. These Philippians had discovered the secret of eternal life: they were aware that their place in heaven did not depend upon anything that they did; it rested solely on what Christ had done for them when he gave up his life on the cross of Calvary.

## Marks of a good teacher

In the third chapter of the letter to the Philippians the apostle speaks to them about the blessing of being 'in Christ'. He begins the chapter with **'Finally,'** but when he says that he does not mean that he has nearly finished his letter. He writes it because he wants his readers to know that he is going to continue with his main message. It means something like: 'Well, as for the rest...' The Greek word he uses is one which is very familiar to my wife and myself. When we are in Greece we often hear our friends, and especially preachers, say, *'Loipon,'* which literally means, 'Well, then...'

When Dr Martyn Lloyd-Jones was preaching and he had come to the end of summing up a great theological statement, he would often pause and then say, 'Very well, then...' This phrase indicated that he was going on to outline the teaching which flowed out of the statement of doctrine he had just made. It meant something like: 'Now, this is what we should do about this teaching...' This is what Paul means when he writes, at the beginning of his third chapter, 'Finally...'

Paul calls the Philippians his **'brothers'** and he commands them to **'Rejoice in the Lord'** (3:1). That was not an easy thing for them to do. They were worried about Paul, because they knew he was shut up in prison in Rome. They were also anxious about their church member, Epaphroditus, who had been sent to Paul and had been very ill. In addition to all of that, they were concerned about their own welfare, but the apostle wanted them to remember that they were 'in the Lord', and therefore they were safe for ever.

What he is going on to tell them in chapters 3 and 4 is something which he had spoken to them about before. It may be that he had said this when he was with them in Philippi. Unlike us sometimes, when we are explaining something to a person who is not really listening, Paul never tired of saying the same things over and over again. So he writes, **'It is no trouble for me to write the same things to you again'** (3:1). The reason why he wants to get these things firmly fixed in their minds is for their **'safeguard'**, because they were in danger.

These people knew that they were on the road to heaven. They had experienced God's salvation. They had been, in simple faith, to the foot of Christ's cross and confessed their sins, and there had been a moment in each of their lives when they had come to believe in the Lord Jesus Christ as their Saviour. But they were surrounded by enemies.

## Marks of the enemies of God

Three times, in the Greek, Paul warns the Philippians to be on their guard. He does this for emphasis. He writes like this because he is convinced that it is so important, and he wants them to take very careful notice of what he is saying.

Paul warns his readers to **'Watch out for those dogs'** (3:2). When we hear the word 'dogs', we think of lovable and affectionate pets, but that is not how the Jews regarded dogs. J. B. Lightfoot explains that there were 'herds of dogs which prowl about eastern cities, without a home and without an owner, feeding on the refuse and filth of the streets, quarrelling among themselves, and attacking the passer-by.'[1]

The word 'dog' was used in ancient times by the Jews to describe all Gentiles, i.e. everyone who was not a Jew. Gentiles, being outside the covenant community, were considered ritually unclean. Jesus recognized the Syro-Phoenician woman as a Gentile. That is why, when she asked him to drive the demon out of her daughter, he replied, 'First let the children [the Jews] eat all they want ... for it is not right to take the children's bread and toss it to their dogs [the Gentiles]' (Mark 7:27). The Lord was not insulting this woman. He was merely making a religious statement and testing her faith.[2] All who were not Jews were considered by them to be ritually unclean. This was because they had not undergone the religious rite of circumcision.

Paul then enlarges more on the people of whom the Philippians should be wary. He tells them, **'Watch out ... for those men who do evil'** (3:2). He has particular men in mind here. It does not seem that Paul is referring in this passage to those selfish Christians about whom he wrote in the first chapter (1:15); those men were at least preaching Christ, even if they had the wrong motives. The people the apostle warns about here are those who 'do evil'. Yet they were claiming to do good. It appears that they were the same men whom Paul spends a great deal of time denouncing in the epistle to the Galatians. These were Jews who were trying to stir up trouble for Paul. They taught that the way to heaven was by keeping the Jewish law, but what they considered to be good works (circumcision and keeping endless religious rules) were, according to the apostle, 'evil' works.

These Judaizers attacked the Christian believers because they trusted in Christ alone for salvation. Paul later goes on to tell the Philippians that these people are living as 'enemies of the cross of Christ. Their destiny is destruction, their god is their stomach, and their glory is in their shame. Their mind is on earthly things' (3:18-19).

The Philippians of the first century AD were not the only ones who needed the warning to be on their guard against these false teachers. Everyone, in any generation, who knows and

loves the Lord must beware of such purveyors of false religion
and of their evil ways.

Thirdly, Paul describes these people as **'those mutilators
of the flesh'** (3:2). Circumcision was introduced into
Abraham's family (Gen. 17:10-14). It was a physical cutting
of the body to show that the members of Abraham's family
(and his descendants) had the mark of God on them. Their
obedience in this matter was a sign that the Lord had made a
covenant with them and had set his seal upon them, and that
consequently they enjoyed a special relationship with him.

These Judaizers, against whom Paul warns the Philippians,
were so proud of their circumcision that they claimed that for
a man to be in a right relationship with God he must be
circumcised. However, Paul could not accept this, particularly
as a council of the apostles who had gathered at Jerusalem
some years earlier had declared that circumcision was not
necessary for salvation (Acts 15). The apostle maintained that
it was by faith in Christ alone that anyone was saved (Gal.
2:14-21). He became so angry with those who continually
agitated about this that he exclaimed, '[If they think mutilating
themselves is so vital, then] I wish they would go the whole
way and emasculate themselves [i.e. remove their sexual
organs]!' (Gal. 5:12).

These false teachers, who were going around the Roman
Empire trying to undermine the teaching of Paul, were only
concerned about the outward act of circumcision. They had
forgotten that the real purpose of this sign was to indicate that
a spiritual transformation had taken place in the life of the
person. Way back in the Old Testament, God had commanded
his people to 'Circumcise your hearts ... and do not be stiff-
necked any longer' (Deut. 10:16). But these religious Jews
were so intent on seeking to destroy the work of Paul and other
Christian leaders that they were not prepared to listen to what
God was telling them through the gospel message.

## Marks of God's people

Paul tells the Philippians, **'It is we who are the circumcision'** (3:3). He means that he and his readers (whether or not they had undergone physical circumcision) were the true chosen people of God.[3] He explains in the epistle to the Colossians that the 'cutting away' which matters is not that of a piece of flesh, but the removal of the sinful nature — not by a knife, but by the blood of Christ which he shed on the cross (Col. 2:11). All those who come to Christ in faith are so completely transformed that they have a new nature implanted within them which leads them away from sinful ways and towards godliness and holiness.

In effect Paul is saying that these men who were so proud of their Jewish rituals had developed a spirit which was contradicting the message of the gospel. They thought that they were God's chosen people, when all the while their objection to Christ and his cross had placed them outside of the covenant of grace. Moisés Silva writes, 'Judaizers are the new Gentiles, while Christian believers have become the true Jews.'[4]

Next Paul gives three ways in which anyone can know that he or she is part of the true circumcision.

First, he says that **'We ... worship by the Spirit of God'** (3:3). He is not talking here about singing hymns and choruses. He is speaking about the way in which we conduct our lives. That is what he means by the word 'worship' in this letter. If we are true Christians, then the whole of our lives must be given over to the glory of God. Paul explains this in writing to the Romans: 'I urge you, brothers, in view of God's mercy, to offer your bodies as living sacrifices, holy and pleasing to God — this is your spiritual act of worship' (Rom. 12:1).

We worship the Lord by the Spirit of God and we worship him by the way we live our lives. Worship is not to be confined

to what we do in church in a formal service. When Jesus spoke
to the woman by the well in Samaria he found that she was
puzzled by religion. This is why she said to the Lord, 'Our
fathers worshipped on this mountain [Gerazim], but you Jews
claim that the place where we must worship is in Jerusalem
[Zion]' (John 4:20). Jesus told her, 'A time is coming and has
now come when the true worshippers will worship the Father
in spirit and truth, for they are the kind of worshippers the
Father seeks' (John 4:23).

Jesus meant that God is not confined to temples built with
hands. Nor is it the method we use to worship God that matters.
It is the kind of people we are that really counts when we seek
to glorify God's name. When Jesus spoke about 'true worshippers' he meant all those who have repented of their sins and
trusted in Christ alone to save them. It is such people who
really worship God and who devote their lives to his glory.
This does not mean that they spend every minute of their days
reading their Bibles or praying or singing. It means that they
seek to live with their hearts right with God and they do their
best to honour him in everything they do, say and think.

The second evidence which Paul gives to show that true
believers are of the circumcision is that they **'glory in Christ
Jesus'** (3:3). People who depend upon religion are usually
those who boast about what they have done, but true Christians
have nothing about which they can boast. They know that they
have been saved by grace through faith, and even that faith has
not come from within themselves (Eph. 2:8-9). It is the free gift
of God.[5] True Christians glory only in Christ and what he has
done for them.

The third piece of evidence that we are the true circumcision is that we **'put no confidence in the flesh'** (3:3). The
Judaizers had put all their hope in the sign of circumcision —
a cut in their flesh. However, Paul, who himself was a very
devout Jew (3:4-6), did not depend on any external act for his

salvation. His confidence was not in ceremonies, good works or 'trusting to luck'. His confidence was in Christ alone, because he knew that all he needed to help him live for God's glory in this life, and take him all the way to heaven when he died, was found in Christ.

Paul knew that mere religion could do nothing to save him. He knew that he could have no confidence in the flesh, and by 'flesh' he meant anything that was not from God. He also knew that there was no hope at all for him unless he confessed that there was no good within him and sought God's continual forgiveness for his sins.

In the same way we need to remember that we do not honour God merely by the amount of Christian meetings we attend each week, or by the number of times we take part audibly in our church prayer meetings. Our personal holiness does not rest on any religious ceremony that we perform, however spiritual that act might be; our spiritual life is increased when we give over the whole of our lives to the worship of God (see Rom. 12:1).

Not only should we live humble, godly lives ourselves, but we should also constantly be on the watch for those who teach that religious observance, without true spirituality, is what is required for godliness. We should oppose these people and also warn other believers about their activities. These present-day 'dogs' often appear in the guise of church leaders who claim to be priests offering sacrifices on behalf of the people, when all the while they are really fouling the footsteps of young and immature Christians.

The shame of the evangelical church today is that we keep quiet while these men do evil and lead people astray from the paths of true spirituality.

# 13.
# Four plus three equals a minus

*Please read Philippians 3:4-7*

If we stop and look back over our lives and consider what we have achieved, we shall recall our successes, or otherwise, at school or in sport. We can look around us and see what kind of home we have put together, how many children we have brought into the world and how we have brought them up. We can consider what we have accomplished in our working lives and what we have attained through our own efforts in our spare time. We can think about what we have done to help other people in the struggles of life and to make this world a happier place to live in.

But what does all that effort really amount to? We can ask ourselves, 'Fifty years after I'm dead, will there be any cause for anyone to remember me?'

In Philippians 3:4-7 we see Paul doing some similar arithmetic. He had been dealing with the attacks of certain Jewish people who had been trying to undermine the church. They claimed that a person must become a Jew before he or she could become a Christian.

However, Paul had countered that argument by telling his readers about the folly of having confidence in anything other than Christ. When the apostle became a Christian on the Damascus road his whole life and thinking were transformed. In the previous chapter of this book we saw that his religion could not save him. In this chapter we are going to examine how Paul illustrates what he means.

In verse 3 he has explained that true believers are those who have 'no confidence in the flesh'. And in case any of his readers thinks he is only saying that out of jealousy, because he himself cannot claim the privileges of being a Jew, or observing the law, as the Judaizers can, he proceeds to outline some details about his own religious life and experience.

Paul was not warning the Philippian church members against these teachers because he resented the advantages they possessed in being Jews. It was not a question of sour grapes. Far from it! Before his conversion Paul had been as devout a Jew as any of his critics. He could honestly say, **'If anyone else thinks he has reasons to put confidence in the flesh** [i.e. in anything other than Christ], **I have more'** (3:5). Or, as he told the church at Corinth, 'If there is any boasting to do, then I, too, can indulge in it' (see 2 Cor. 11:21).[1]

The apostle goes on, in verses 5 and 6, to detail all of the qualifications which the Jews laid down as things which would commend a person to God. He listed four things which he inherited from his parents, then he added three others which he had achieved through his own efforts. Finally, he worked out the sum total of all his many advantages in being a devout Jew. The surprising thing was that all of these points in his favour (the pluses) came, not to seven (which for the Jews is symbolic of perfection) but to nothing — in fact, they came to less than nothing; they amounted to a minus.[2]

On the Damascus road, when the light of God shone into his soul and he came to know the Lord Jesus Christ as his Saviour, Paul made the discovery of the truth of Jesus' words when he said, 'What good will it be for a man if he gains the whole world, yet forfeits his soul?' (Matt. 16:26). He realized that, despite all of his religiosity, without Christ he was lost.

But let us examine his advantages.

## What Paul had inherited from his parents

They had made sure that he had been **'circumcised on the eighth day'** (3:5). This marked him out as a Jew, and one who had been brought up to be a very devout member of the Jewish community. Circumcision was the rite for which the Judaizers contended more than anything else. Even today, no man can become a Jew until he is circumcised. This was what set the Jews apart from all of the other nations. It was the special sign which God gave to Abraham (Gen. 17:12) and all Jews were proud of it.

Not only had Paul been circumcised, but this had taken place on the eighth day of his life (3:5). The eighth day was the exact day that God had laid down on which boys were to be circumcised, and this was observed by all pious Jews (Gen. 17:12; Lev. 12:3). Abraham's other son Ishmael (the child of the bondwoman), was not circumcised until he was thirteen years old (Gen. 17:25), and Jewish proselytes — those who take on the Jewish faith later in life — are not circumcised until their manhood; but Paul could hold up his head and claim to have been circumcised on the eighth day of his life — just as the Scriptures had laid down

His second claim to blessing was that he was **'of the people of Israel'** (3:5). Israel was the name which had been specially given to Jacob by God after he had wrestled with God (Gen. 32:28).[3] This was the name of which the Jews were particularly proud. The Ishmaelites (the ancestors of today's Arabs) can also trace their descent back to Abraham, but only those of Israel (Jacob's descendants) can claim to belong to God's special people. Hywel Jones says, 'Israel was the dignified name for the people of God.'[4] Paul was proud that he came from such solid stock.

The third blessing which Paul mentions was his descent from **'the tribe of Benjamin'** (3:5). Benjamin was one of the smallest of the tribes of Israel (Ps. 68:27), but this tribe claimed to enjoy special privileges. Benjamin was the son of Jacob's favourite wife, Rachel. When Joseph was visited by his brothers in Egypt, it was Benjamin that he wanted to see most of all. This was because all the rest of Jacob's sons were his half-brothers (Gen. 42:20). Benjamin was also the only son to be born in the land of promise (Gen. 35:16-18).

A further reason why Benjamin was considered to be a very important tribe was that Israel's first king was a Benjamite (1 Sam. 9:1-2). In fact Paul may have been named after this king, for his Jewish name was Saul (see Acts 9:1-31; 13:2,9). The apostle could also claim special status as a Benjamite because the tribe of Benjamin had remained loyal to the dynasty of David after the division of the kingdom (1 Kings 12:23). In addition, the city of Jerusalem and its temple lay within the territory of this tribe (Judg. 1:21). The tribe of Benjamin also occupied a position of honour when the army of Israel went into battle (Judg. 5:14; Hosea 5:8). It is not surprising, therefore, that Paul considered belonging to this tribe to be a privilege.

The fifth blessing which Paul inherited from his parents was that he could claim to be **'a Hebrew of Hebrews'** (3:5). By this he meant that he was a Hebrew born of Hebrew parents.⁵ The Jews were spread all over the known world of those days. There were tens of thousands of them in Rome, and there were more than a million in Alexandria, in Egypt. Almost all of these Jews kept to their own religion and their own customs.

It was, naturally, necessary for them to speak the languages of the people round about them in everyday life. Greek was the language most widely spoken among the educated people, and as time went by very many of the Jews failed to keep up their use of Hebrew. This was because they did not need to use it. Since they had a Greek version of the Old Testament they did not even need Hebrew in order to carry on worshipping God and carrying out the rituals of their religion.

However, Paul and his family were not among those who forgot their Hebrew. When Paul told the Philippians that he was 'a Hebrew of the Hebrews', he meant that he had kept up his Hebrew language and all of the culture which sprang from it. That would have required a great deal of effort—especially as he was born and brought up in Tarsus, which was outside of the borders of Israel (it is now in modern Turkey).

Paul was taught Hebrew at home and sent by his parents to Jerusalem as a young boy (Acts 22:3). He was very fluent in the Jewish languages of both Hebrew and Aramaic (cf. Acts 21:40; 22:2; 26:14). He was a Hebrew Jew and not a Hellenistic one (cf. Acts 6:1). [6]

So anyone who tried to argue with Paul by saying that he did not know what he was talking about, on the questions of circumcision and the observance of the Jewish law, had clearly failed to take into account all these privileges which Paul had inherited from his parents. But there was more to come.

### What Paul had gained by his own efforts

We now turn to consider all that Paul had done before his conversion in an attempt to enhance his religious standing before God and his fellow men and women. **'In regard to the law,'** he was **'a Pharisee'** (3:5). We tend to think of the Pharisees as wicked people, because in the Gospels they were often scheming to trap Jesus. But the majority of them led very strict and holy lives. The name 'Pharisees' means 'the separated ones'. They were called by this name because their aim in life was to try to please God by refraining from all things which they considered to be impure. They demonstrated this by keeping the commandments very meticulously.

Paul had grown up with a great desire to put God first in his life. The Judaizers who criticized him could not fail to be impressed with his claim that in regard to the law he was a Pharisee.[7] He himself told King Agrippa that the Jews who had known him all his life could testify 'that according to the strictest sect of our religion, I lived as a Pharisee' (Acts 26:5).

Having explained his efforts in regard to keeping the law, Paul then went on to speak of his **'zeal'** for God (3:6). He had demonstrated this by **'persecuting the church'**. Because he was a strictly religious Jew, he had expended a great deal of time and energy in defending his own religion from what he saw at the time as the threat of Christianity. He tells the Galatians, 'I was advancing in Judaism beyond many Jews of my own age and was extremely zealous for the traditions of my fathers' (1:14).

As a young man, he became so incensed because the followers of Christ were trying to overthrow the Jewish religion that he set out to destroy them. Luke tells us that he breathed out murderous threats against the Lord's disciples (Acts 9:1). He himself told Agrippa that he became 'convinced that [he] ought to do all that was possible to oppose the name of Jesus of Nazareth' (Acts 26:9). This was when he went to the high priest and obtained letters from him, enabling him to arrest any who belonged to 'the Way' and to take them as prisoners to Jerusalem (Acts 9:2).

The final claim that he could make to demonstrate that he could have confidence in the flesh — if anyone could — was that **'as for legalistic righteousness'**, he was **'faultless'** (3:6). Paul was not saying that he had never committed any sins. He had come to realize that no human being could lead a totally sinless life (only the Lord Jesus Christ was completely free from sin). But so far as outward observance of all the commandments and the rules laid down by the Pharisees was concerned, he was blameless. He had been like the Pharisee in the parable which Jesus told in Luke 18:9-14, who stood up in the temple 'and prayed about himself: "God, I thank you that I am not like other men — robbers, evildoers, adulterers — or even like this tax collector. I fast twice a week and give a tenth of all I get,"' or like the rich young ruler who told Jesus, 'All these [commandments] I have kept since I was a boy' (Luke 18:21).

## What all of this added up to

In the eyes of Judaism the four privileges which Paul had inherited from his parents and the three evidences which he gave of his religious devotion all added up to a great deal of righteousness. But so far as Paul was concerned, they all amounted to nothing. In fact they came to less than nothing! They totalled a minus. He said, **'I consider them rubbish'** (3:8). This was because, in the meantime, he had come to know the Lord Jesus Christ as his Saviour.

While he was travelling to Damascus a very bright light shone on him and he fell to the ground. Then the Lord spoke to him and he was completely transformed. As a result, he too became a follower of Jesus (Acts 9:3-6). However, he never forgot that he had once been so zealous for his religion that he did all he could to persecute the church. He said, 'I am the least of all the apostles and do not even deserve to be called an apostle, because I persecuted the church of God' (1 Cor. 15:9). He was so ashamed of his actions that he could never regard them as a positive point in his favour; rather he saw them as minus points weighing against him. He says, **'Whatever was to my profit I now consider loss for the sake of Christ'** (3:7). He now knew that he could not gain God's blessing through his own righteousness.

To illustrate what he meant, we can recall the time when Paul was being taken as a prisoner to Rome and they were sailing during the autumn on one of the small Roman trading ships (see Acts 27). The ship was loaded with a cargo of grain. The merchants hoped to make a good profit from the sale of this grain. However, when a storm blew up and the ship was danger of being wrecked, the crew threw the precious cargo overboard in the hope of saving the ship. The goods which they had hoped would be a source of profit to them had now become a liability and it was only by the sacrifice of them (or by turning their hoped-for gain into loss) that the lives of those on board were saved.

This is an important lesson for us all. Whatever it is that seems to be for our profit will have to be considered a loss compared with the surpassing greatness of knowing Christ Jesus (3:8). Knowing him personally (not just knowing about him) is what matters far more than the sum total of our religious ritual and beliefs. A good Christian upbringing can become a real disadvantage if we are relying on that to win salvation for us.[8] It is only through trusting in the shed blood of Christ and his death on the cross that anyone can gain genuine righteousness.

# 14.
# Knowing Christ personally

*Please read Philippians 3:8-11*

In 1949 a young American college student called Jim Eliot was preparing to go out on the mission-field. At that time he wrote these words: 'He is no fool who gives what he cannot keep to gain what he cannot lose.'

Some seven years later he was sitting with four friends deep in the Ecuadorian rain forest. They had gone to this remote spot in an attempt to make contact with a very secretive tribe called the Auca Indians.

On Sunday morning, 8 January 1956, one of these young men radioed to their base that there were promising signs that their efforts were going to be successful and that they hoped to send further news shortly. They then sang together their favourite hymn, 'We rest on thee, our Shield and our Defender'. Those at base waited and waited for further news, but none came.

Many months later they learned what had happened to these five young servants of God. Elisabeth Eliot (Jim's wife) tells the story: 'By four-thirty that afternoon the quiet waters of the Curaray flowed over the bodies of the five comrades, slain by the men they had come to win for Christ, whose banner they had borne.' She continues, 'The world called it a nightmare of tragedy. The world did not recognize the truth of the second clause in Jim Eliot's credo: "He is no fool who gives what he cannot keep to gain what he cannot lose.""[1]

Many centuries before the murder of these missionaries, Paul showed that he had the same attitude as Jim Eliot when he wrote to the Philippians, **'Whatever was to my profit I now consider loss for the sake of Christ... I consider them rubbish, that I may gain Christ'** (3:7,8).

## What Paul lost

When he became a Christian Paul lost everything he had once held dear. He had been very proud of his religious heritage. Before his conversion he rejoiced that he had been born into a family where the traditions of the Jews were held in high esteem. He was well pleased with what he had achieved in his own religious devotion to God. He had a great enthusiasm for everything which had to do with his Jewish traditions, and he was determined to see that the law of Moses was upheld by himself and everyone he could persuade to keep it.

In those days he had held his Jewish religion so dear that he had depended upon it to gain him acceptance with God. No one could say that he was a slacker in his zeal for the Lord and his commandments. He was not one of those people who are quite happy to let others do all the hard work. He was prepared to undergo all kinds of trials and deprivations in order to win God's favour.

He was even prepared to sacrifice time which he could have used to earn money. He demonstrated his eagerness by setting out on a journey to Damascus with the express intention of rooting out as many of the early Christians as he could find and bringing them back to Jerusalem for trial. He wanted them punished, and his strong desire was that the new 'religion of

Jesus' should be eradicated altogether. But God had other plans for him. Paul became a Christian on that road to Damascus. There he underwent a complete change. He was now prepared to lose all the things which formerly he had counted as being to his profit. He declared that they counted for nothing, so far as God was concerned.

He even added up all of his achievements and said that they were a loss for the sake of Christ. This was because he now had a new Master; the Lord had shone into his soul with the light of his gospel and Paul's whole thinking had been completely transformed. He no longer slavishly followed his former religion of works. He realized that there was nothing he could do to justify himself and earn God's righteousness. Formerly he had considered that he was blameless before God because he had kept all the rules and regulations of Judaism impeccably. But since he became a believer in Christ he said, **'I consider them rubbish, that I may gain Christ and be found in him, not having a righteousness of my own that comes from the law'** (3:8-9).

Paul could say this because he had discovered that no one can become righteous by his own efforts. He realized that he had not understood the real purpose of the law of God, which he thought he had been keeping all his life. Instead he discovered that the law only serves to prove that 'There is no one righteous, not even one' (Rom. 3:10). He realized that all his religious efforts amounted to nothing more than rubbish and were fit only to be thrown away.

This word which is rendered 'rubbish' in modern Bible versions can mean 'dung' (as it is translated in the Authorized Version), but it can also refer to 'the refuse or leavings of a feast' — i. e. the food which is thrown away from the table. The Judaizers spoke of themselves as honoured guests seated at the Father's table enjoying a banquet, while they referred to the Gentile Christians as dogs greedily snatching up the refuse meat which fell from the table. However, Lightfoot tells us that Paul reverses the image: 'The Judaizers are themselves the "dogs" (3:2) [and] the meats served to the sons of God are spiritual meats; [while] the ordinances, which the moralists value so highly, are the mere refuse of the feast.'[2]

Paul gladly turned his back upon all the things which once he considered so vital to please God. He counted them as less than nothing because he had discovered that 'The very commandment that was intended to bring life actually brought death' (Rom. 7:10). When he cried out, 'What a wretched man I am! Who will rescue me from this body of death?' he was able to give the answer: 'Thanks be to God, my deliverance has come, not through legalistic effort, but through Christ' (see Rom. 7:24-25).


## What Paul gained

He gained a person, a Saviour, one whom he called **'Christ Jesus my Lord'** (3:8). Paul, or Saul as he was known in those days, came to know the Lord Jesus Christ when he was on the road to Damascus and on the way to destroy the believers there. The Lord Jesus himself appeared to him and asked him, 'Saul, Saul, why do you persecute me?' Saul replied with another question: 'Who are you, Lord?' The Lord answered: 'I am Jesus, whom you are persecuting... Now get up and go into the city, and you will be told what you must do' (Acts 9:4-6).

Following this, Saul was blind for three days, during which time he neither ate nor drank anything (Acts 9:9). When he and his companions reached Damascus God appeared to a believer there called Ananias and told him, 'This man [Saul] is my chosen instrument to carry my name before the Gentiles and their kings and before the people of Israel. I will show him how much he must suffer for my name' (Acts 9:15-16).

Ananias must have been a very gracious man because Saul had acquired a reputation as a hunter of Christians. Ananias may have known that it was Saul who had looked after the clothes of those who stoned Stephen to death (Acts 7:58). He certainly knew who Saul was and why he had come to Damascus (Acts 9:13-14). However, despite all his natural fears, Ananias believed God's word which declared that Saul had been chosen to be a servant of the Lord.

As a result of his conversion Paul could call Jesus **'my Lord'**. This was because he had come to know the Lord Jesus Christ in a very personal way. Before he had become a Christian he had carried out all his religious observances in the hope that God would give him his general approval, but since he had met with Christ he had come into a personal relationship with him. If we can understand what a tremendous thing that was, then we shall understand why he said, **'I consider everything a loss compared to the surpassing greatness of knowing Christ Jesus my Lord'** (3:8).

Paul had often tried to please God through his own efforts but in the end he came to see that all of these amounted to less than nothing. The vital matter of his sin, which had lain like a great barrier between him and God, had been taken away on the road to Damascus. There he had experienced the saving power of the Lord Jesus Christ and had become a new man because Christ had paid the price of his redemption when he died on the cross. Christ had been the bridge which had brought Paul to God. It was not Paul's upbringing which had done it; nor was it his religious works which had brought him salvation. It was his faith in Christ which opened up the way to God. This is why Paul adoringly calls Jesus 'my Lord'.

The apostle was given **'a righteousness ... which is through faith in Christ — the righteousness that comes from God and is by faith'** (3:9). When he was converted his eyes were opened so that he saw that Christ was the only one who had ever kept the law perfectly and, therefore, it was only Christ's righteousness which had any value in God's sight. However, the incredible thing was that God gave his Son to die on the cross as his free gift to make undeserving sinners righteous. Paul realized that the only way that sinners can obtain Christ's righteousness is by accepting it by faith (just like any other gift, it can only be accepted, not earned).[3] Paul illustrates this further when he writes to the Corinthians, 'God made [Christ] who had no sin to be sin for us, so that in him we might become the righteousness of God' (2 Cor. 5:21). In other words, on the cross Christ took our sin (and our unworthy righteousness) upon himself, and instead he gave to us (imputed to us) his only pure righteousness.

Many years after Paul's time Count Zinzendorf expressed the same truths in these words:

Jesus, thy robe of righteousness
My beauty is, my glorious dress;
'Midst flaming worlds, in these arrayed,
With joy shall I lift up my head.[4]

Before this Paul had exercised faith in his own observance of the Jewish religion, but he had received no assurance of salvation through these things. He discovered what each of us has to find out — that the only way in which any of us can receive the forgiveness of our sins is by putting our faith in Christ. Faith in religious upbringing, valuable as such an upbringing is, cannot save us. Faith in religious ceremonies, helpful as they can be, can never earn us eternal life. Faith in good works, important as they are, cannot open up the way into heaven for us. It is only as we put our trust in the Lord Jesus Christ alone, and as we seek him, that we can be granted that gift of God's righteousness.

**What Paul longed for**

The apostle never ceased to praise God for saving him, but he realized that he could not stand still spiritually. He was very elated because he knew Christ personally, but he wanted to know him better. In verse 10 he tells the Philippians, **'I want to know Christ.'** Of course, he already knew Christ. In fact he had already said that knowing Christ Jesus as his own Lord and Saviour was something which surpassed all knowledge (3:8). Dr Martyn Lloyd-Jones compares him to 'a dog straining at a leash' in his longing to know even more of Christ.[5]

When a girl falls in love she is excited that she has, at last, met 'the light of her life'. She does not say, 'Well, I'm in love with him, but I don't want to know anything more about him.' She wants to find out as much as she can about the man and show her love for him more and more.

It was the same with Paul and his love for the Lord. He was so filled with Christ that he wanted to know him in a better and richer and fuller way. He did not say, 'I want to have a great knowledge *about* him.' Nor was his desire to know more truths about the Saviour. Although that was all true, it was not his main concern. What he longed for, more than anything else, was to have a greater and more intimate knowledge of his Lord and Master. Just as Adam knew Eve, when they had been banished from the garden of Eden (Gen. 4:1, AV), so Paul wanted the experience of the Damascus road to become more intense.

That ought to be our desire also. Those of us who can really say that Jesus is ours should not be content to think, 'Well, I'm a Christian now. That's all there is to it.' We should want to know him better and we should constantly be seeking the Holy Spirit's aid to lead us into closer fellowship with God. There is an old hymn which sums this up very well:

More about Jesus would I know,
More of his grace to others show;
More of his saving fulness see,
More of his love who died for me.

More, more about Jesus,
More, more about Jesus,
More of his saving fulness see,
More of his love who died for me.[6]

However, Paul did not only want a more profound relationship with Christ; he actually wanted to be like Christ. He desired to experience **'the power of [Christ's] resurrection'** (3:10). Think of the tremendous strength that was exerted to raise Jesus from the dead. Paul tells the Philippians that he wanted to experience that power in his own life. He did not want it so that he could do great miracles and show off his abilities. He had no selfish ambition (see 2:3). What he longed for on his own account was what he prayed for on behalf of the Ephesians — that they might know the incomparably great power which God exerted when he raised Christ from the dead (Eph. 1:19-20). He craved that power in his own life so that he could be identified with Christ and live and witness for him.

Secondly, he wanted to know **'the fellowship of sharing in [Christ's] sufferings'** (3:10). Christ suffered on the cross to save his people, and Paul did not want to escape any experience which would help him to know Christ better. He even wanted to suffer for the sake of Christ. All through his Christian life Paul experienced many sufferings. He tells us about some of them in 2 Corinthians 11:23-33.

Thirdly, the apostle wanted to become **'like'** his Master **'in his death'** (3:10). Jesus had told his disciples, 'If anyone would come after me, he must deny himself and take up his cross daily and follow me' (Luke 9:23). Taking up one's cross meant dying, and dying very painfully. Paul wanted so much to become like his Saviour that he was prepared even to die in his cause. This does not mean that he necessarily wanted to be crucified. What he longed for was to be prepared to die daily, if need be, for the sake of Christ (1 Cor. 15:31).

Finally, Paul wanted to reach his goal. It was his hope that he might **'somehow ... attain to the resurrection from the dead'** (3:11). When he talked about the power of the resurrection in verse 10 he meant power for living. But here he is speaking about being raised from the dead. We should note that he does not say, 'I want to be raised from *death*', but, 'I want to be raised from *among the dead.*' He is speaking about a specific occasion — the last day. To the Thessalonians he writes, 'The Lord himself will come down from heaven, with a loud command, with the voice of the archangel and with the trumpet call of God, and the dead in Christ will rise first' (1 Thess. 4:16).

Paul's great ambition was to be among that number who will be raised on the last day with Christ (1 Cor. 15:23). In other words, the apostle longed to go home to heaven when all his work was done. His great desire was to be with the Lord for ever (1 Thess. 4:17). That ought to be our deepest longing too.

# 15.
# Pressing onwards

*Please read Philippians 3:12-16*

Do you ever become discouraged and feel that you are not making any progress in your Christian life? Perhaps you look at other Christians and see them as shining examples of Christlike living, and then you look at yourself and realize that you are far behind them in holy living. The harder you try to honour the Lord and be an influence for good, the more difficult it seems to succeed.

Paul was a great man of faith, yet he writes, **'Not that I have already obtained all this** [holiness], **or have already been made perfect...'** (3:12). As he wrote to the church at Philippi he knew that not everything was going smoothly there. He was aware that some people were criticizing his teaching because he taught that the old Jewish ceremonial law did not save anyone. He was also conscious that some of the church members had been drawn away from the faith; they had listened to those who taught that everyone had to become a Jew before he or she could be a Christian.

However, Paul did not look down from a great height upon the church at Philippi and say, 'I've arrived at full maturity. If you don't want to follow me, then you had better go on your own way.' Instead he told them what the situation was in his own life. There was one thing which he desired more than anything else in the world. That was 'to know Christ and the power of his resurrection and the fellowship of sharing in his sufferings, becoming like him in his death' (3:10). He meant that he had not yet achieved that, but he was not going to give up trying to reach that goal.

Did the apostle mean by this that he was uncertain about his own salvation and he was constantly striving to earn it? Not at all. That is the first thing I want us to notice in this chapter.


## Paul was secure

He knew that he was safe for ever because, as he told the Philippians, something had happened in his life: **'Christ Jesus took hold of me'** (3:12). He does not mean by this that there came a time when he realized that he needed something in addition to his humdrum existence. He viewed his salvation as much greater than that. He knew that if it had been left to him, he would never have sought the Lord. Up to the time of his conversion he had been trusting in his strict obedience to the Jewish law to gain him a place in heaven, but he had come to see that faith in religious observances gained him nothing (3:7-9).

He realized that his salvation did not depend upon anything that he had done, or that he continued to do. He knew that his redemption rested solely on the Lord Jesus Christ and what Christ had done for Paul when he shed his blood as a sacrifice for sin on the cross of Calvary. That is why the apostle put the whole of his salvation down to Christ's death. Jesus died to pay the price of Paul's sins, and not only of Paul's sins, but those of all who come to Christ in repentance and faith.

Paul was so filled with the wonder of what Christ had done for him that he did not even mention the fact that he had repented of his sins and put his trust in Christ for salvation. In this verse he puts his whole emphasis on this truth: 'Christ Jesus took hold of me.'

Christ first took hold of him when he was travelling on the road to Damascus. Earlier in this book reference has been made to that story. On that day Paul, or Saul as he was known then, set out with one aim in view. He was such a zealous Jew that he was determined to smash the new religion of the Way. But God had other ideas. The Lord did not get angry at Saul's audacity and say, 'I am going to destroy this man for wanting to do such an awful thing.' Instead Christ took hold of him and told him, through the mouth of Ananias, 'The God of our fathers has chosen you to know his will and to see the Righteous One and to hear words from his mouth. You will be his witness to all men of what you have seen and heard' (Acts 22:14-15).

Paul emphasized the sovereignty of God when he said that Christ took hold of him. The expression also implies that the Lord held on to him with a very firm grip. In fact, that grip was so strong that nothing was ever able to make Christ let go. That is how Christ takes hold of every believer. When he truly saves us, we can be sure that we remain his for ever. Jesus himself said of those who are truly converted to him, 'I give them eternal life, and they shall never perish; no one can snatch them out of my hand' (John 10:28). It is no wonder that Paul was so certain of his salvation.

When this happens to a person, Satan does not just give up and go away. He uses all kinds of things to try to make the Lord loosen his grip upon his people. But even our sins will not cause Jesus to let go of us once he has us in his grasp. Of course, it saddens him greatly when a Christian fails him. However, just as the Lord called Peter back to his side after he had denied knowing him, so he calls us back to his fold when we fall into sin. This is another reason why Paul was so certain of his salvation. We too should continually praise God for his constant love for us.


## Paul had his eye on a goal

Although Paul was completely safe in Christ's kingdom, yet he still longed for even more blessing. He had 'arrived' in the sense that he had been saved, and he knew that he was safe for evermore, but he was aware that there was more to being a Christian than just the initial experience of coming to faith in Christ. He wanted to press onward to what was ahead. He desired to take hold of that salvation for which Christ had taken hold of him. In other words, although he knew he was safe for ever, he realized that he had not yet been made perfect.

Paul is not saying in this passage that it is possible to reach a state of sinless perfection while we are still on this earth. He knew well enough that no one, except the Lord Jesus Christ, could ever achieve that. One of the reasons why he knew that was so was because sin was constantly dogging his footsteps. Nevertheless, he knew that one day, when he reached heaven, he would be free from this body of sin and death for ever. Then, in glory, he would be perfect.

However, for the time being, Paul was not perfect. But he did not give up. He pressed onward, with the intention of winning **'the prize'** (3:14). He uses one of his favourite figures of speech at this point and draws on the imagery of athletics to illustrate a spiritual truth. As we saw in an earlier chapter, he often uses this picture (1 Cor. 9:24; 2 Tim. 4:7; Acts 20:24). He has already spoken about this great prize in verses 7-11. There he said that he wanted to know Christ and the power of his resurrection and the fellowship of sharing in his sufferings. He desired to become like him in his death and then to attain to the resurrection of the dead (after he had left this earth).

Paul knew that God had called him heavenwards for that ultimate purpose. In athletics the prize is not awarded before the race is completed and, therefore, it can only be looked for after the finishing-line, and not before it.[1] At the end of each of those great races in the games of ancient Greece there was always great excitement. Those who were near the finishing-line could see who had reached it first. But there was more to winning than just personal satisfaction. There was always someone very important waiting on the platform to give out the prizes after the race. A great hush would suddenly fall on the whole crowd who had been watching. Everyone would be waiting to hear, booming around the stadium, the name of the person who had won. Finally the announcement would come and the name of the winner would be called out. At that moment all the spectators would burst out into thunderous applause as the victorious athlete went forward to receive his reward. This is the picture Paul has in mind when he says, **'I press on towards the goal to win the prize for which God has called me heavenwards in Christ Jesus'** (3:14). Paul was eager to hear his name called on that great day.

## Paul was straining towards that goal

In order to win that prize the runner, or the charioteer, had to keep his eyes on the goal, or finishing-tape. Only citizens of Greece could take part in those races: they were not open to just anybody. That is one of the points that Paul is making here. He is not saying that in order to be saved a person has to run in a race and come first, ahead of everyone else. His point is that no one can even make a start in the Christian race until that person has been born into God's kingdom. On the other hand, all those who are true believers should be running the Christian race. The Lord requires that each and every Christian should keep the finishing-line steadily in view. All should be eagerly longing to win the prize.

However, there are some differences between the earthly picture and the spiritual truth it illustrates. First of all, in an earthly race there can only be one winner, but the Christian race is very different. In Christ we can all be winners (just as all who compete in the London marathon receive a medal). This means that every believer should be straining towards the goal, or finishing-line. We, as believers in the Lord Jesus Christ, should run as athletes run (1 Cor. 9:24).

Secondly, the prize which those ancient Greek athletes gained was a wreath made of leaves. It was a very great honour to win it, but it eventually faded away and died. Our reward is so different; it is far better than that: the crown which we shall receive at the end of our Christian lives will last for ever (1 Cor. 9:25). That crown is the Master's 'Well done, my good servant!' (Luke 19:17). It is the 'crown of righteousness, which the Lord, the righteous Judge, will award ... on that day ... to all who have longed for his appearing' (2 Tim. 4:8). It is 'the crown of glory that will never fade away' which will be given by the chief Shepherd (1 Peter 5:4).

## Paul exerted great determination

If we are going to be winners for Christ, then there are a number of things we must do. First, we must be determined to win. This is why Paul says, **'One thing I do'** (3:13). He did not allow himself to be distracted from his mission. Nothing would put him off from the task to which God had called him. He took no notice of Satan. He did not listen to those who wanted to divert him by engaging him in time-wasting intellectual discussions about philosophy. He had his eyes on the goal.

Every believer should take very careful note of Paul's attitude. We too should be single-minded in our devotion to Christ. We should allow none of the excitement which is going on in various churches to distract us from our pilgrim pathway. We should not be drawn into the discontent that so many Christians are engaged in. Satan is delighted when believers start murmuring and losing interest in the work of the gospel. Neither should we be like so many who are tired and say they cannot make it to the Bible Study and prayer meetings of the church. Very many people in these days seem to lack that vital quality in the Lord's work which I call 'stickability'. Let us allow none of these things to divert us from our task. Let us be like Paul and say, 'This one thing I do.'

The apostle uses very strong language here: **'Straining towards what is ahead, I press on towards the goal to win the prize'** (3:13-14). Each of us should seek to work for the Lord with that same kind of determination. The picture here is of the runner reaching his hands as far forward as they will go, straining every nerve, in order to reach the winning-post first. He must make sure that he does not look back to the failures of his past life. Instead he must exert all his strength as he continues to make progress in his Christian life, knowing that the Lord has declared of his people, 'I ... will remember their sins no more' (Jer. 31:34). Much ground has already been covered, and this knowledge spurs him on in his effort to reach the winning-post. He runs, knowing that he is not labouring on his own; the God who has called him heavenwards is also giving him strength and grace in Christ Jesus to attain his goal.

Paul continues by telling his readers to be disciplined in their Christian lives: **'All of us who are mature should take such a view of things... Let us live up to what we have already attained'** (3:15). There were obviously some at Philippi who disagreed with Paul, but he does not wave his big

apostolic stick at them. He says, quite simply, **'God will make
[it all] clear to you.'**

We should exercise great determination in our desire to live
for God's glory. There were many in the Bible who failed to
do this. Lot had so much going for him, but he lost sight of the
goal. Samson judged Israel for twenty years, but he preferred
the embrace of Delilah, and so he finished his life blind and
bound. Saul had the honour to be the first King of Israel, but
he became disobedient to God and he was finally rejected by
the Lord. Think of Ananias and Sapphira: they were both
members of the early church, but they lied to God because of
their greed. And God took their lives from them.[2]

We should do our best to make sure that none of us ends up
like any of these people; instead let us take our example from
others. Take Joseph, for instance. He had a much harder time
than any of us have had. Yet he pressed on despite the unfair
circumstances of his life. He kept his hope firmly fixed on the
Lord. Or think of Daniel. He was a captive in a foreign land,
cut off from the temple, yet he determined to remain faithful
to God and his laws. Then, in the New Testament, we find great
encouragement in the experience of John Mark. He stumbled
at one time as a missionary and Paul refused to take him with
them, yet he recovered his vision for the spread of the gospel.
Then Paul was glad to have him as one of his helpers once
more.

If anyone reading these verses is feeling discouraged just
now and life does not seem worth living, you should remember
what Paul tells us here. We should keep our eyes on the
finishing-line and think about the prize of the high calling of
God in Christ Jesus. We must forget what is behind and press
onwards to what is ahead. We should stretch out our hands to
grasp that prize which Christ gained for us upon the cross of
Calvary.

# 16.
# Keep your eyes open

*Please read Philippians 3:17-21*

Everyone who is in the public eye has to be very careful how he or she behaves. Many politicians have had their careers ruined because of their immoral or dishonest behaviour. Sadly, few of them resigned voluntarily because they had committed an 'indiscretion'; most of them only gave up their office when the matter became public and caused embarrassment to their political party.

Every believer must always remember that 'There is nothing concealed that will not be disclosed, or hidden that will not be made known' (Luke 12:2). Church leaders especially are required, not only to lead godly lives, but to set an example to other believers on how they should live and react to the trials of life. Paul told the Corinthians to follow his example, as he followed the example of Christ (1 Cor. 11:1), and here he tells the Philippians to **'Join with others in following my example, brothers, and take note of those who live according to the pattern we gave you'** (3:17). The pastor of a large church in our town wrote to me this striking sentence: 'Our job as Christian leaders is to set a good example.'

Paul reminds all believers that they should keep their eyes open. They should observe and copy those who are reliable teachers of the Christian message. They should also avoid those who are enemies of God's truth. At the same time, all true

Christians should be eagerly looking for the coming of the Lord.


## Observe God's people

We must be careful whose example we follow. There are many who call themselves Christians, but they are not behaving as they should. We can assess the true characters of people by the way they conduct themselves. If a man says he loves animals and yet, when no one is looking, he kicks the cat, then quite obviously he is lying and does not love animals at all. He is merely saying he does because he thinks that is the politically correct thing to say.

Over 300 years ago, John Owen wrote these words about the religious condition of England: 'In many places it is useless to seek for Christianity among Christians.'[1] That is a very sad indictment of Britain at the time that Owen was writing, but if that was true all those years ago, then it is certainly true today. When discerning Christians look around them and see the way this country is moving, then tears spring to their eyes and their hearts are filled with a deep sadness.

The people whom we should observe closely, and want to copy, should be those who truly love God. We can tell if they love God by looking to see whether they live in ways which please him. Paul was one who gave the whole of his life over to glorifying the Lord. He allowed nothing to interfere with his aim of wanting to know Christ better (3:10). He wrote to the Philippians, urging them to follow his example.

The example which Paul set was one of putting Christ first. He had no confidence in the flesh (3:3). Nor did he have any reliance on his own abilities to save himself. He knew that his only hope of salvation lay in trusting Christ alone. He gloried in knowing Christ Jesus as his Lord (3:8) and he lived his life pressing onward to win the prize for which God had called him heavenwards (3:14).

However, Paul was not saying, 'Look, what a wonderful man I am!' Elsewhere he calls himself the worst of sinners (1 Tim. 1:15). Despite that, he rejoiced that God had shown him mercy and had saved him with his everlasting salvation.

There were other fine Christian leaders whom the Philippians knew personally. Paul said that they should aim to live according to the pattern which he and these other men set before them. They were to model their own behaviour on those **'who live according to the pattern we gave you'** (3:17). Among these others were Timothy and Epaphroditus, about whom he had written in chapter 2. He says to the Philippians, 'Look at these friends and at me.' They were also to follow the pattern set for them by the Lord Jesus Christ. Peter tells us, 'When [those who arrested Jesus] hurled their insults at him, he did not retaliate; when he suffered, he made no threats. Instead, he entrusted himself to him who judges justly' (1 Peter 2:23).

The apostle wanted the Philippians to have that same kind of attitude. The way they lived should follow that pattern. He tells Timothy, 'Set an example for the believers in speech, in life, in love, in faith and in purity' (1 Tim. 4:12). We should each ask ourselves, 'Where do I look for a pattern of holy living?' Do we look to well-known bishops and theologians? Do we look to certain worship-group leaders who tour the country singing? Or do we look to those who are leaders in the church to which we belong?

We should also ask ourselves, 'What kind of example am I giving to other people — especially to the young?' Do you want them to copy your behaviour? If the way we live is not according to the pattern of the apostles, then we need to make some radical changes in our lifestyle and outlook.

## Watch out for the enemies of Christ

We should not even listen to, let alone copy, those who are the
enemies of the cross. Such people are leading God's children
astray. In the days of Paul there were many who did this. They
were everywhere. Paul was so concerned about them that he
had often warned the Philippians about them. These people
were influencing the church at Philippi in a bad way. They
were not just a nuisance. They were alive and active. We know
this because Paul says, **'Many live as enemies of the cross of
Christ'** (3:18).

Their presence, and what they were saying and doing, made
Paul extremely unhappy. It affected Paul badly that these
people were openly living as enemies of the cross of Christ, but
he did not get into a tearing rage over them. Neither did he start
denouncing them and trying to have them banned from society. Instead he wept over them. He was deeply grieved because
they had misunderstood the meaning of the cross. He longed
that they might come to see in the cross of Christ the only way
to be delivered from their sins, and he was very concerned lest
they should be a bad influence on the believers at Philippi.

So many people today are living as enemies of the cross of
Christ. A great number of them would call themselves Christians. If they talk about the cross at all, they merely say it was
an example of love. They have missed the point entirely. It is
true that Christ died as an example to us that we should even
be prepared to lay down our lives for our friends. The Bible
tells us these things about the cross, but the cross of Christ
means so much more than that. The death of Christ in such a
cruel way was not something that went wrong. It was all in
God's plan and purpose. He knew that the only way any of us
can get to heaven is by having our sins washed away in the
precious blood of Christ.

Those who deny the atoning death of Christ are not merely opposed to the cross; they are actually living, day by day, as enemies of the cross. Paul wanted the Philippian believers to live according to the pattern he had set them (3:17); these people who were antagonistic to the cross lived in a different atmosphere and had entirely different motives.

The apostle then proceeds to give us a vivid description of these enemies of the cross. He says, first, that their end is destruction (3:19). Whatever they thought about religion, they were going to end up in hell. By saying, **'Their destiny is destruction,'** Paul did not mean that they would just cease to exist. Jesus talked about hell as a place of everlasting punishment (Matt. 25:46) and Paul tells the Thessalonians that those who do not know God 'will be punished with everlasting destruction and shut out from the presence of the Lord and from the majesty of his power' (2 Thess. 1:9).

Does that not frighten you? It ought to. If you do not know for sure that you are saved, then this fact alone ought to drive you to Christ because he is waiting to receive anyone who comes to him in simple trust. And if you do know him as Saviour, then it ought to make you want to lead all of your friends and relatives to seek God's salvation. Time is short, because the destruction which these enemies of the cross will experience is beginning even in this life.

A second thing Paul tells us about these enemies of the cross is that **'Their god is their stomach'** (3:19). That is what they worship. They have no time for the real God. They are only interested in physical gratification. They worship what gives them satisfaction. There are people like that today. Those who go to church to be noticed, or in the hope of receiving something that makes them feel good, are in some ways like these people. No one should attend church just to receive a blessing. Each one should come to church to bow in humble and loving worship, in the company of others, before the God of the universe.

Thirdly, Paul tells us that **'Their glory is in their shame'** (3:19). These people were proud of the way in which they behaved. They thought it was a clever thing to speak about the cross in a derogatory way. Instead of regarding this as something to be proud of, they should have been thoroughly ashamed of themselves. They were like those mentioned in the letter to the Hebrews who were 'crucifying the Son of God all over again and subjecting him to public disgrace' (Heb. 6:6).

Finally, we are told concerning these enemies of the cross that **'Their mind is on earthly things'** (3:19). This was because they refused to have the mind of Christ (2:5). Instead their minds were controlled by their sinful nature. This nature is described in Colossians 3, where Paul tells his readers, 'Set your minds on things above, not on earthly things.' They were told to 'Put to death ... whatever belongs to your earthly nature: sexual immorality, impurity, lust, evil desires and greed, which is idolatry.' But these enemies of the cross refused to obey these injunctions. They were not willing to 'rid [themselves] of ... such things as these: anger, rage, malice, slander and filthy language from [their] lips' (Col. 3:2,5,8). Instead they set their minds on earthly things — not caring that the sinful nature cannot please God (Rom. 8:8). That is why Paul describes them as enemies of the cross of Christ.


**Look for your Lord**

Paul had urged the Philippians to follow the example of good leaders. Then he told them to avoid those who are enemies of the cross. He now follows that up by telling them to look upwards. Those of us who know, love and serve the Lord

remember our citizenship. We know that our real home is not
on the earth; it is in heaven.

The Philippians would have understood the symbolism
which Paul was using because, as we saw in the opening
chapter, Philippi was a Roman colony. It was a long, long way
from the Imperial City. However, even though it was in Greek
territory, it still belonged to Rome. Its citizens wore Roman
dress. It was governed by Roman magistrates. Latin was
spoken. Roman justice was administered. Roman morals were
observed, and even the earth was considered to be Roman
ground. So, when Paul tells the Philippians, **'But our citizenship is in heaven'** (3:20), he is in effect saying, 'Just as the
Roman colonists never forget that they belong to Rome, you
must never forget that you are citizens of heaven, and your
conduct must match your citizenship.'[2]

In writing about heaven Paul found his thoughts directed
towards his Lord. Everything the apostle did and said reminded him of the Lord Jesus Christ in the same way that every
activity of our lives should also remind us of our Saviour.
Thinking about heaven reminds us that we **'eagerly await a
Saviour from there, the Lord Jesus Christ'** (3:20). Just as
we should live our lives like a runner who is straining every
nerve towards the winning-tape (3:13), so we eagerly await
our Saviour from heaven. This means that the glorious return
of our Lord should occupy much of our attention. The Second
Coming of Jesus is mentioned over 300 times in the New
Testament, so we should never forget that he is coming again.
We should be living our lives in ways which please him.

If we are still alive when Jesus returns, what would we want
him to find us doing when he comes again? If we ask ourselves
that question, it will make us take care how we live our lives,
because we do not know when he is coming back. We should
note how godly people live. We should not copy the way the

enemies of Christ live. And we should be careful how we live because Christ is coming again and 'Everyone who has this hope in him purifies himself, just as he is pure' (1 John 3:3). In view of his return we should be looking away from all sinful pleasure as we await his manifestation in glory (1 Cor. 1:7; Col. 3:4).

When Christ returns he will come with a mighty power and **'everything'** will be put **'under his control'** at that time (3:21). No longer will people ignore or reject him. His great power will force all people to their knees and on that day they will confess that 'Jesus Christ is Lord' (2:11).

When he comes, he **'will transform our lowly bodies so that they will be like his glorious body'** (3:21). This is something which we find too much to take in: our lowly bodies of sin and death will be transformed by Christ's power (the Greek word used here is transliterated 'dynamite'). Paul tells us about this in 1 Corinthians 15. When that happens all the pain, all the filth, all the anxiety, all the trouble will be taken away from us and we shall be transformed and made like Christ's glorious body. John tells us, 'When he appears, we shall be like him' (1 John 3:2). This is something which transcends our understanding, but it is nevertheless a glorious fact that, if we have been born again, at that time the transformation will be complete and everything about us will be radically changed and 'conformed to the likeness of his Son' (Rom. 8:29).

# 17.
# Internal conflict:
# the great enemy of the church

*Please read Philippians 4:1-3*

If in one hundred years' time, your name was to be discovered mentioned in an old document, what one thing would you like the finder to learn about you? Would you like it to be recorded that you were a very kind and loving person, or that you were a mature Christian, or that you were good at making people feel at ease?

Two ladies from the church at Philippi have gone down in history, and the thing they are remembered for is that they had fallen out with each other. No one today knows what these women disagreed about. Paul does not say what the problem was, although presumably everyone else in the church at the time knew what they had quarrelled about. It must have been festering for some long time, because Paul had heard about it in faraway Rome, and he was so concerned that he found it necessary to mention it in his letter, and actually to name the two ladies.

Internal troubles of this kind can flare up very quickly. I think I once heard of a church where there had almost been a split in the membership over the colour that the kitchen had been painted. The complaint was that the deacons did it without consulting the membership of the church. Sometimes difficulties have arisen over trivial matters such as who has taken the flowers home at the end of the day's worship.

All such incidents tend to cause unhappiness to the other members of the church and, even more importantly, these conflicts impair the church's witness in the community. The sad thing is that most of these altercations arise out of selfishness. They happen because the people concerned do not have the same attitude that Christ Jesus had (2:5). James picks up the same theme when he asks, 'What causes fights and quarrels among you?' He gives the reason: 'Don't they come from your desires that battle within you? You want something but don't get it' (James 4:1-2).

We should heed the warnings of Scripture. As church members we must do our best to make sure that we do not come into conflict with our fellow believers. The devil still finds work for idle hands to do, and sometimes troubles of this sort arise in a church because some of the members have too much spare time on their hands. Instead of gossiping to their fellow-Christians, they should occupy their time in positive ways. Some Christians enjoy a good argument; these friends should always make sure that the end result of the debates in which they engage is profitable to all and glorifying to God.

Three hundred years ago John Owen said that divisions over minor matters had caused Christianity to lose much of its authority in the world. This is even more true today than it was when he wrote it. It is, therefore, not surprising that many people fail to take notice of what the church says. Owen concludes, 'Christians ought to be a blessing to everybody. But they are not.'[1]

It saddens me that in these days we can regularly read articles and letters in religious magazines written about all kinds of puerile matters which stem from a lack of love for those whose views differ slightly from those of the writers. Satan delights to see this kind of thing happening. He loves to see Christians at one another's throats. We should do our very best not to get caught up in this kind of 'nit-picking', which gives the Evil One so much pleasure.

Paul addresses these things in our passage. He has been writing to the Philippians about how Christians should live. He has expressed his desire that they should live according to the pattern which he had given them (3:17). He certainly did not want them to live as enemies of the cross of Christ (3:18). Instead they were to live as citizens of heaven (3:20), keeping in the forefront of their minds the fact that Christ is coming again to this earth (3:21).

If we are going to be those who obey the Lord and contend for the faith of the gospel, then we should recognize that we are engaged in a bitter fight with Satan and the world. Disunity among us is a flaw in our armour.[2]

## Live, remembering vital truths

If we are to be strong Christians in a strong church, then we must know the truths of God's Word and stand firm in them. Paul often exhorted his readers to **'Stand firm'**. Earlier in this epistle he writes, 'Whatever happens, conduct yourselves in a manner worthy of the gospel of Christ. Then, whether I come and see you or only hear about you in my absence, I will know that you stand firm in one spirit, contending as one man for the faith of the gospel' (1:27). To the Corinthians he writes, 'Stand firm. Let nothing move you. Always give yourselves fully to the work of the Lord, because you know that your labour in the Lord is not in vain' (1 Cor. 15:58). A little later, he tells them, 'Be on your guard; stand firm in the faith; be men of courage; be strong. Do everything in love' (1 Cor. 16:13).

But the problem is that the devil does not want us to stand firm. He longs for us to be unsure of what we believe. He rubs his hands with glee when we do not know how to put these beliefs into action, and he is keen to promote disagreements among us, because one of his chief aims is to stain the good name of the church. He does not want the Lord's people to be firm in the faith. His concern is that they should be weak and ineffective. If we are falling out with one another, then we shall be impotent in our evangelism. However sound we may be in the truth of the Bible, we shall achieve little if we do not love one another — and show it.

However, it is not always easy to 'stand firm'. This is a phrase which in ancient times was used of a soldier in the heat of battle. Sometimes he would receive the order to 'stand firm'. He would be given this instruction when the enemy was surging down upon him.[3]

Whenever I read about the trench warfare of the First World War, and remember what my father told me about it, I shudder. How could those generals, way back behind the front line, order thousands of men 'over the top' into the murderous teeth of the Germans' machine-gun bullets? But they did. Even though there were no guns in the first century, the Roman soldiers knew what it was to face the enemy. They realized that they had to obey the orders given to them. When they were told to charge, then they had to do so, and when they were told to stand firm, then they had to do that, even though they faced almost certain death.

That is what Paul means when he urges the Philippians to **'Stand firm in the Lord'** (4:1). They were to remember that the Lord was their strength and help, and they were to trust in him, come what may. It is the same for us today. We must obey our Captain's orders; that is what it means to behave as Christians. So how can we find the strength to stand firm like that?

First of all, *we are to see that we live according to the pattern Paul gave*. We are to live selfless lives. We are to do nothing out of selfish ambition or vain conceit, and we are always to remember that we should be humble and consider others as better than ourselves (2:3).

Secondly, *our attitude should be the same as that of Christ* (2:5). He, who left heaven's glory and came to this earth, humbled himself and took on the form of a servant (2:7). So, instead of standing up for our rights, and arguing for our own views, we should be like Jesus and be prepared to wash the feet of our fellow believers (John 13:5,14-15).

If Euodia and Syntyche had remembered and obeyed those things, then they would not have fallen out with each other, and Paul would not have had to cause them embarrassment by mentioning their names in this letter (see 4:2-3).

Thirdly, *we must remember that Christ is Lord.* What is it that every tongue will confess on the last day? It is that Jesus Christ is Lord (2:11). The apostle did not ask that these ladies agree for Paul's own sake, or even for the good of the church (although both of those would have been valid reasons for doing so). No, he urges them to **'agree with each other in the Lord'** (4:2).⁴ If only we recognized the lordship of Christ over our lives, and over our churches, then we would not be so foolish as to fall out with our fellow believers.

## Live, resolving present quarrels

Things could not carry on as they were. This display of disunity was affecting the whole church. You cannot have two ladies in a church who refuse to speak to each other, or each of whom regards everything the other one does with suspicion. This kind of thing immediately causes division in the whole church. People begin to take sides in the argument, whispering starts and certain people refuse to work with certain others.

Incidents of this kind are a disgrace. They bring dishonour to the church which Christ loved and for whose sake he gave himself (Eph. 5:2). They use up a great deal of energy which ought rather to be expended in the work of the gospel. They also get the church a bad name because we can be sure that the people of the world will hear about the quarrel. Bad news travels fast and is certain to reach the people you would rather did not hear of it.

## Something needs to be done

It is very helpful to see how Paul handles this situation. Firstly, he says something must be done about it. When problems are allowed to carry on, without any attempt to resolve them, then things are liable to go from bad to worse. That is why Paul addresses this problem in the letter.

## Paul's love for the Philippians

Secondly, he demonstrates very clearly that he still loves the Christians at Philippi, despite this dreadful blot on their copybook. Notice all the terms of endearment he uses. There are six of them in verse 1 alone.

First, he calls them **'my brothers'**. He does not use his apostolic authority. He does not even say, 'As an elder, I command you to sort this matter out.' No, he says, 'I write to you as one brother to other brothers.'

Secondly, he tells them he loves them: **'you whom I love'**.

Thirdly, he says, **'whom ... I long for'**, and he follows this by calling them **'my joy'**. He has continually expressed much joy in this letter, and every time he thought about the church at Philippi he prayed for them with joy (1:4).

Fifthly, he says they are his **'crown'**. He does not use the Greek word *'diadema'*, which refers to the crown worn by a king. The word he uses is *'stephanos'*, which is that for the crown won by victorious athletes at the games (cf. 3:14; 2 Tim. 2:5). This word was also used for 'the crown with which guests were crowned when they sat at a banquet, at some time of great joy'.[5] Perhaps a modern equivalent might be when we put on paper hats at the Christmas dinner table as a symbol of our joy and celebration.

Paul ends this first verse with the sixth term of endearment, **'dear friends'**. Can we doubt that he loves them, even though he is about to give a rebuke to two of their members? He knows that 'The thick cushions of love and trust will absorb the impact of his rebuke.'[6]

## Paul's refusal to take sides

The third point that we should note about the way in which Paul handles this situation is that he refuses to take sides in this disagreement. He does not say, 'I plead with Euodia and with Syntyche.' He says, **'I plead with Euodia and I plead with Syntyche'** (4:2). He pleads with both of them equally, and he uses very loving terms. He does not say, 'Sort this matter out, or I'll come there myself and knock your heads together!' He tells them, 'I plead with you.'

Surely these ladies must have been ashamed of their behaviour when they saw that the great apostle Paul had stooped down and urged them to agree with each other in the Lord. What he told them in effect was: 'You are both in the Lord. Now live as sisters in Christ, and enjoy all the benefits of peace and harmony that there are in the gospel.'

## Praise for their hard work

Fourthly, he praises them for their past hard work. These two sisters had both put much effort into the cause of the gospel. They had actually worked with the apostle in seeking to build up the church at Philippi. Perhaps they were among the women whom Paul had found worshipping God by the riverbank on his first visit to Philippi (Acts 16:13). Certainly he says that they had **'contended at [his] side in the cause of the gospel'** (4:3). They had been very bold in speaking to non-Christians about the salvation that there was in Christ, but now it seems that they would not even speak to each other.

*Unity in the gospel*

Finally, Paul seeks to resolve this problem by urging other
church members to help these women to be friends again. He
specially addresses one whom he describes as a **'loyal yoke-
fellow'** (4:3). There is much speculation on who this might
have been. Some think that it was Epaphroditus, the man who
was bearing this letter back to Philippi (2:25). Others suggest
that 'yoke-fellow' is actually the name Syzygus and that Paul
was referring to a man of this name. Whoever he was, he was
a real person and he was asked (not ordered) by Paul to assist
these women to be in agreement with each other as they had
been in the past. His name is very significant because a yoke
is what was used to bind two oxen together when they were
ploughing a field or working a grinding-machine. The animals
were fixed to each other with a piece of wood called a yoke,
and this ensured that they moved together at the same speed
and in the same direction.

This is what is required when it comes to preaching the
gospel. Paul had already urged the Philippian church to
contend 'as one man for the faith of the gospel' (1:27). Now
once again he tells them to work as a team. There can be little
success in evangelism if people are busy gossiping about one
another and everyone is pulling in opposite directions. So he
encourages them to use their energies to pull together for the
sake of the gospel.

Clement and others were contending at Paul's side for the
cause of the gospel and these women too were to do likewise.
Unity of purpose is important in the church, but it must not be
unity at the expense of any vital belief or practice; we must also
follow the teaching of the Bible. The only things which must
be sacrificed are unhelpful ones such as selfishness and face-
saving. God's plan is that all his people 'agree with one
another so that there may be no divisions among [them] and

that [they] may be perfectly united in mind and thought'
(1 Cor. 1:10-12).

## Live, mindful of your heavenly destiny

Paul had already reminded the Philippians that their citizenship is in heaven (3:20). So, if they were citizens of heaven,
why were they quarrelling among themselves? Had they lost
sight of heaven? In that blessed place there are no tears or
bitterness. Therefore, the question for each of us is: 'How can
we live as citizens of heaven if we are at odds with a fellow
believer?'

The apostle reminded all the believers at Philippi that their
eternal destiny was heaven. They already knew this because,
for each of them, there had been a time in their lives when they
had repented of their sins and put their faith in Christ. They
knew that their entrance tickets were waiting for them, with
their names written on them. Each of these fellow workers had
been purchased by Christ when he shed his blood on the cross
of Calvary on their behalf.

That was not all. Their names had been written in **'the book
of life'** (4:3). This book is the register of the people of God
(Exod. 32:32,33). In it are recorded the names of the righteous
(Ps. 69:28). Come what may, every person whose name has
been written in God's book will go at last to heaven (Isa. 4:3;
Rev. 3:5;13:8; 17:8). The Lord Jesus told his disciples to
rejoice above all else that their names were written in heaven
(Luke 10:20). [7]

# 18.
# God's cure for worry

*Please read Philippians 4:4-7*

There are many things which cause us to worry, and most of us wish that we did not do it so much. Worry can lead to a whole range of illnesses and sometimes seems to get right inside us, so that we can scarcely think about anything else other than the difficulty which is causing us so much disquiet.

This kind of thing is not a new phenomenon; it happened in Bible times as well. In the passage we are now considering Paul goes right to the root of the problem of anxiety when he talks about **'your hearts and your minds'** (4:7). It is the heart and the mind which so easily, and so quickly, get out of control. This happens on those occasions when we go to bed, put out the light, turn over and then, instead of going to sleep, find that all kinds of issues start going round in our heads.

Our minds are active because we are anxious about something we have done, or have not done, or have to do when we get up in the morning. Because we are full of anxiety, our hearts and our minds are extremely active. We start thinking about the problems we face. It is then that the heart takes over. For example, we may remember a little child who we know is very ill. As we lie in bed, unable to sleep, our hearts go out to that helpless little one and to the parents.[1] Or we may be concerned about some old friend who does not seem to want to have anything more to do with us; that makes us very sad and even angry. In cases like these I have just quoted, all the time that we are trying to get off to sleep our hearts and minds are darting here and there and keeping us awake. We are full of disturbed thoughts and emotions and feel we would do anything to experience the peace which will enable us to drift off to sleep. At times like these we long to be like the psalmist who said, 'I lie down and sleep' (Ps. 3:5). We have no difficulty in lying down, but when we do so we find that we cannot sleep because there are so many problems weighing heavily on our minds and hearts.

The Philippians would certainly have had very many things to worry about, which would no doubt have kept them awake at night. For one thing, they belonged to a young church which was being opposed by those who were the enemies of the cross (3:18). Then there were the problems caused through the selfishness of some of their members (see 2:3). Their great desire would have been that Paul could come and sort out the matters which were causing them disquiet. In the past he had always been such a strength to them, but now he was shut up in prison, and they did not even know whether he would ever come out of the prison alive (see 1:13,19-26). So we can have no difficulty in imagining why the Philippians were filled with anxiety, why they had no peace. We can also see why the apostle deals at this point with this question of anxiety, which held them in its icy grip,[2] and why he tells them God's cure for worry.

Paul does not say, 'Don't worry about it; it may never happen.' That kind of advice is seldom helpful. Instead he issues them with three difficult commands. First he commands them to be full of *joy* at all times; secondly, they are to be full of *gentleness*; and finally, they are to be full of *prayer*. He then assures them that if they obey these orders they will discover that the peace of God will guard their hearts and minds and keep them from all the attacks of the Evil One.

## Be full of joy at all times

**'Rejoice in the Lord always'** (4:4). How could they rejoice when they had so much trouble? They were not just being selfish and thinking of their own troubles; they had in mind Paul's imprisonment; they were anxious about the well-being of Epaphroditus (2:25); and they were concerned about the state of their witness in the face of so much opposition from the various kinds of enemies who surrounded them.

However, the apostle knew about all of these things, and yet he still commanded them to rejoice. He had already spoken of joy on several occasions in this letter. In the first chapter, when he mentioned those who were preaching Christ out of wrong motives, he had concluded by saying, 'Christ is preached. And because of this I rejoice. Yes, and I will continue to rejoice' (1:18). When he reminded them that he was ready to die for Christ he encouraged them to rejoice with him: 'I am glad and rejoice with all of you. So you too should be glad and rejoice with me' (2:17-18). And at the beginning of chapter 3 had told them, 'Rejoice in the Lord!' (3:1).

The amazing fact is that there was nothing which could stop this man from being glad that he was counted worthy to suffer for the sake of Christ. He invited Timothy to join with him in suffering for the gospel (2 Tim. 1:8) and he had already told the Philippians that he wanted to share in Christ's sufferings and become like him in his death.

Why was he telling them these things? Because if they wanted to have peace in their hearts and minds they must remember that joy is not dictated by a person's surroundings. The same applies to Christians today. Our circumstances alter from time to time, and we know that it is easy to be happy when we are enjoying good health and have a good bank balance. However, it is not so simple to rejoice when we have been summoned to see a consultant at the hospital — or the bank manager! But Christian joy does not depend on our changing circumstances. It depends on the one who does not change.[3]

The circumstances of this life can depress us because we do not know what awaits us around the corner. The fear of the unknown is one of the greatest causes of our anxiety, but the Lord Jesus Christ is so different from anyone on earth. He never changes: 'Jesus Christ is the same yesterday and today and for ever' (Heb. 13:8). If we put our trust in him we need never be cast down. Isaiah said, '[God] will keep in perfect peace him whose mind is steadfast' (Isa. 26:3). When we read that scripture we may say to ourselves, 'That is all very well for people who feel stable, but I'm anything but stable. How can I attain that kind of stability?' Isaiah gives us the answer. He tells us about the kind of person who has a mind which is steadfast: 'Trust in the Lord for ever, for the Lord, the Lord, is the Rock eternal' (Isa. 26:4).

If we are to rejoice in the Lord always — and Paul emphasizes this command by adding, **'I will say it again: Rejoice!'** — then we must look away from ourselves. True Christian joy, which leads to the absence of worry, is not inward-looking. It does not concentrate on thinking about our own happiness (that is selfishness, which Paul tells us to avoid). Joy is directed towards pleasing God. Jesus taught his disciples not to worry: 'Do not worry, saying, "What shall we eat?" or "What shall we drink?" or "What shall we wear?"' He tells his followers that our heavenly Father knows that we need these things. Instead of worrying about them, the Lord tells us to 'Seek first [God's] kingdom and his righteousness, and all these things will be given to you as well' (Matt. 6:31-33).

If we are going to rejoice in the Lord, then we must turn away from ourselves and our own needs. We have to thank God for all his provisions for us, and we have to be concerned about the needs of others (see 2:3). That is what Christ did, and we should endeavour to follow his example.

## Show gentleness towards everyone

**'Let your gentleness be evident to all'** (4:5). On the face of it, this seems a strange thing for Paul to say. How can showing other people that we are gentle help to cure us of worrying?

The first thing to notice is that this Greek word is one which is used of the Lord Jesus Christ. Paul appealed to the Corinthians 'by the meekness and gentleness of Christ' (2 Cor. 10:1). Although Jesus was always gentle in his dealings with other people, he was not weak. He knew what was right, and nothing would move him from that conviction. Gentle as he was, he had no qualms about overthrowing the moneychangers' tables in the temple (Matt. 21:12). This was because they were turning his Father's house into a den of thieves. The Lord did not spend precious time and energy in frustration over this awful behaviour. He stepped in and did something about it.

If we are to be freed from the overwhelming burden of anxiety, then we too should seek to behave like Christ. He was never angry at the wrong time, but he was *always* angry at the right time. He knew what was right, and he did it. However, he always acted in a gracious way. We should never hesitate to tell the truth, even if it might be hurtful to the person to whom we are speaking, but, as those who seek to be like Christ, we should always seek to temper our words with gentleness, so that they do not give so much offence that the wrongdoer fails to alter his behaviour for the better. Paul tells us that we should always speak the truth, but we should do it in love (Eph. 4:15).

When the apostle commanded the Philippians to 'let [their] gentleness be evident to all', he was using a word which has a very broad range of meaning. It has been translated in various ways. L. H. Marshall gives us a very helpful definition of it. He says that it is best summed up as 'fair-mindedness'. Others translate it as forbearance, yieldedness, geniality, kindliness, sweet reasonableness, considerateness, charitableness, mildness or magnanimity. It is 'the attitude of a man who is charitable towards men's faults and merciful in his judgement of their failings because he takes their whole situation into his reckoning'.⁴

If we want to take God's route to freedom from worry then we should never brood over the wrong that others may do. When a church disciplines one of its members, the elders should never go around with a smug, self-satisfied air, giving the impression that they are pleased with themselves because they have done the right thing and acted in accordance with the Word of God. Instead they should be full of sadness because, although they have done what needed to be done, it has been a very painful experience for them and the whole church.

If we have to correct someone we should always act justly, but we should let our magnanimity be shown to everyone. All through the Scriptures, we read about God's justice, but also about his mercy. These twin attitudes should be evident in everything that we do.

Another reason why the Philippians were encouraged to 'let [their] gentleness be evident to all' was that **'The Lord is near'** (4:5). It is one of the great sources of comfort to the believer that he experiences the presence of God with him every moment of the day. When he has a difficult task to perform he knows that he does not do it alone; the Lord is near him. When he receives a lovely surprise he does not enjoy it on his own; the Lord is near and shares in the joys with him. And when a believer is loaded down with pain and grief he does not carry that burden on his own either; he knows that the Lord is near him, upholding him in his pain.

Not only should the knowledge that the Lord is present with us help to free us from worry, the Lord is also near in the sense that his coming back to earth is not far off. That was the great hope of the early church; so, if his return was near for them, who lived nearly 2,000 years ago, it is even nearer for us. Paul has just reminded the Philippians that they should be eagerly awaiting the Lord, who will come back in transforming power (3:20-21). If we are bowed down with care we too should remember that soon all of this anxiety and strain will be over for us. We shall then enjoy the beauty and blessing of his presence for ever. Whether we die and go to be with him in glory, or he returns to this earth before that, we shall be with the Lord for ever (1 Thess. 4:17).

Paul also told the Philippians that they were not to be anxious about anything at all. When our hearts and minds are stirred up it is natural for us to be very worried because we cannot see a way out of our predicament. But Paul says, **'Do not be anxious about anything'** (4:6). Peter too tells us what to do with our cares. He says, 'Cast all your anxiety on [God] because he cares for you' (1 Peter 5:7). Many years before this the psalmist had said something similar: 'Cast your cares on the Lord' — no one else can really help — 'and [then you will most certainly discover that] he will sustain you' (Ps. 55:22). Our God is so great that, not only is he interested in us, but he can actually do something about our problem. He can, and will, bear away each and every one of our burdens if only we will come to him and throw our cares on him (just as a little boy casts a stone into the middle of the river). We need never be afraid to cast our cares upon God, because nothing is too great for his power to accomplish. Neither is anything too small for his love to be concerned about.

## Be absorbed in prayer to God

**'Do not be anxious ... but in everything, by prayer and petition, with thanksgiving, present your requests to God'** (4:6). The Lord knows how we are feeling. We may be in such a bad state that worry is getting us down so much that we feel stifled. Paul tells us how to behave in such circumstances. He says that we must be prayerful. That means we must direct our thoughts and desires towards God. If we want to be free from worry we must stop thinking about ourselves and our needs. We are not to be anxious 'about *anything*'. Instead we are to be prayerful. Our motto ought to be: 'Worry about nothing; pray about everything.' Charles Swindoll suggests that we turn our 'worry list' into a 'prayer list'. He advises us to 'Commit each one of those issues that agitate, frighten or burden [us] into God's hands.'⁵

Paul has a number of things to say about prayer. First of all, he uses the general word for 'prayer'. This is a word which means coming into God's presence. Therefore, instead of growing anxious, let us turn to the Lord in prayer. We often meet people who say they do not believe in God, but when they find themselves in a desperate situation they admit that they pray. If we want to know freedom from worry, let us not just call out to God in emergencies. Let us turn to God in prayer about everything that happens to us.

The apostle next talks about 'petition'. That means 'asking for things'. God is able to supply needs. John Newton, the converted slave-ship captain of 200 years ago, wrote about prayer:

Thou art coming to a King;
Large petitions with thee bring.
For his grace and power are such,
None can ever ask too much.⁶

However, we must remember that when we ask for things it must be in a spirit of 'thanksgiving'. If we are not thankful to God for all he is and does, then we are not approaching him in the right spirit. Hendriksen says, 'Prayer without thanksgiving is like a bird without wings: such prayer cannot rise to heaven, can find no acceptance with God.'[7] So we must not be ungrateful in our dealings with God.

The final word Paul uses for prayer is 'requests'. This means that we should pray for specific matters. A lady who belonged to a church where I was the minister often used to recall a time when she was a student. One day she was waiting at a bus stop in the pouring rain and carrying a large pile of heavy books. She prayed hard to the Lord: 'Please, Lord, send a bus. I'm late, and I'm getting soaked.' Soon afterwards she was thrilled to see a bus coming along towards her, but then her heart sank when she saw the number of the bus. She used to say, 'The Lord sent the wrong bus!' What she really meant was that she had not been specific in her prayers. When we pray for missionaries, for example, we should not just pray for God to bless all the missionaries in Africa. We should pray for particular missionaries, using prayer letters to help us pray more intelligently about their situations.

If we rejoice in the Lord whatever our circumstances, if we remember that he is near, and if we turn away from our own selfish desires and seek God in prayer, then we shall discover that we have within us **'the peace of God'** (4:7), and that peace will defy all explanations. The people around us will not be able to understand why we are so peaceful inside. It is because we are experiencing the peace of God which passes all understanding.

Paul knew that peace, even though he was prevented from travelling to see his friends in order to help with their problems; even though there was a strong possibility that at any moment he might be taken outside his prison cell and executed. He could rejoice because he was free from undue anxiety, and he experienced a deep and lasting peace dwelling within him. Just as a sentry was constantly manning the door of his prison, so the peace of God was continually guarding his heart (controlling all his emotions) and his mind (pervading all his thinking).

The wonderful thing is that every believer in the Lord Jesus Christ can know that same peace. It does not come from within ourselves. It comes to us directly from God. It is the peace of God. It belongs to him, and he graciously imparts it to us. That is why it is so wonderful. If we would only turn away from ourselves and our own concerns, then we too could have this peace as our own. We need to cast aside all those things that have been getting us down and turn to God, trusting in him to deliver us from all our fears. We should be those who rejoice in the Lord and his goodness to us in all the circumstances of our lives. And then we shall be able to get on with this business of living our lives for the glory of God.

# 19.
# Be good citizens

*Please read Philippians 4:8-9*

The word 'school' conjures up various pictures for all of us. I did not like school very much. The reason for this may have been because my first five years of formal education took place during the years of the Second World War, when everything, including teachers, was in short supply. I can still visualize the classroom where we were taught. It was at the front of the ancient building, just behind the front wall of the school. In the grounds, overlooking the road, was a sloping board. We all knew that we had to keep looking at this to see if it had changed colour. If it did so then we would all have to put our gas masks on because it would mean there had been a gas attack.

I can see myself now, sitting near the front of the class, slightly to the left of the teacher, chanting, 'Whatsoever things are true, whatsoever things are honest, whatsoever things are just, whatsoever things are pure, whatsoever things are lovely, whatsoever things are of good report; if there be any virtue, and if there be any praise, think on these things' (Phil. 4:8, AV). The beautiful language of the old English version of the Bible burned deeply into my mind. Although I did not quite understand the meaning of the words, I knew they were a kind of code for living. The wonderful thing is that I have never forgotten those words, and I realize that I should aim to live my life by the standard they set.

This kind of teaching, and that of the Sermon on the Mount, are great to aim at but, as Paul pointed out to the Philippians, however hard we try, we discover that we often fail to live according to these principles. It will not be sufficient, on the Day of Judgement, to stand before God and say that we have lived righteously (see 3:8-9). Even those who have been cleansed from their sins in the precious blood of Christ are still required to make every effort to live holy lives. Throughout this epistle Paul has been teaching the Philippians that they are citizens, not just of Philippi, but of heaven too (3:20) and they must live lives worthy of that kingdom.

It is unlikely that, before they knew Christ as their Saviour, they were all villains or criminals. Most of them would have been brought up to observe a strict moral code of behaviour. They were required to lead a good life, thinking of other people and, above all, honouring their rulers. It is the same with many people today. If someone is not a true believer in the Lord Jesus Christ that does not necessarily mean that he or she lives a totally immoral life. The standard of morality seen in the lives of many non-church-goers is very high indeed. They lead such upright lives that other people often remark about them, 'What a good Christian he (or she) is!'

In these two verses Paul seems to be saying, 'Now you know how you ought to live, but I am telling you that in every part of your life your standard of conduct must be better than that of the pagan world around you. Now that you belong to Christ you are required to live as citizens of heaven.' To encourage them to live upright lives, Paul tells them that they must get their thinking right (4:8) and make sure their behaviour is right (4:9). These things go together. If they think and act correctly, then they will be rewarded with a personal knowledge of the God of peace (4:9).

**Right thinking**

All our behaviour begins in our minds. How we think deter-
mines how we act. The great nineteenth-century preacher
C. H. Spurgeon wrote, 'God will not live in the parlour of our
hearts if we entertain the devil in the cellar of our thoughts.'[1]
This means that if we think unhelpful, selfish and wicked
thoughts, then our behaviour will certainly be influenced by
those thoughts and, unless we are checked, we shall end up
doing wrong things.

The apostle Paul tells the Christians at Rome, 'Those who
live according to the sinful nature have their minds set on what
the sinful nature desires' (Rom. 8:5). In other words, if you are
living in wrong ways, it is because you are thinking wrong
thoughts. No one commits criminal acts without having first
thought about and planned such things. Terrible sexual deeds
against children start initially in the minds of the perpetrators.
Therefore, we should make sure that we do not think about evil
things, however attractive the devil attempts to make them.

The reverse is also true. If we think good, wholesome and
right thoughts, then it is much more likely that we shall act in
right ways. Most, if not all, of us have to admit that, however
hard we try, sinful thoughts do keep coming into our minds. So
what can we do to get rid of those things? We need to face up
to the matters which tempt us. If we are easily tempted to read
filthy magazines, then the best way to avoid temptation is not
to lift our eyes in the direction of the top shelf at the newsagents
(which is where such things are usually placed). If necessary,
we should even avoid entering such shops.

The sure way to keep sinful thoughts, and those things
which disturb our inner peace, out of our heads is to concentrate on those matters which are good.[2] That is Paul's injunc-
tion here, and it explains why he carries on with the list which
he started back in verse 4 of this chapter. There he told the

Philippians, and us, to rejoice in the Lord. We are to be gentle in the sight of everyone. We are not to be anxious about anything, and we are to pray always.

The apostle begins this verse with a word which he had already used at the beginning of chapter 3, the word **'Finally'**. As we observed before, Paul did not say this as a device to keep the attention of his audience, in the hope of stopping their minds from straying. He was so taken up with writing to his dear brothers and sisters in Christ that it almost seems as though he found it difficult to draw the letter to a close. But he knew he must end it soon, so he wrote the Greek word *'loipon'*, which in modern Greek has the sense of 'Well, then...', or 'So...' In other words, Paul is saying, 'For the rest...', or 'Furthermore...', rather than, 'This is the last thing I am going to write.'

Then Paul once again addresses the Philippians as **'brothers'** (cf. 3:1; 4:1). Obviously he was worried about the disunity among them. This was why he urged Euodia and Syntyche to agree with each other in the Lord (4:2). Nevertheless, despite all of their shortcomings, the people in the church at Philippi continued to be Paul's brothers, because both he and they were united together in Christ. None of the problems which beset them could ever prevent them from being Paul's brothers.

He then gives them a list of virtues which he wants them to strive after. Each of the first six things he prefixes with the word **'whatever...'** He means, 'It doesn't matter what your situation is, or how you are feeling; this is what I want you to do. I want you to put these excellent matters into practice.'

He speaks first about those things which are **'true'** and **'noble'**. These are realities. That is what truth actually is; it is something which is real. There is nothing insincere or sham about truth and noble living. Paul does not merely want them to accept these things; his earnest desire is that they should take these matters very seriously indeed. This is the kind of attitude

which Paul tells Timothy and Titus to look out for in elders and
deacons and older men. He says that they should 'be temper-
ate, worthy of respect, self-controlled' (Titus 2:2).

Next he urges the Philippians to do their utmost to do that
which is **'right'** and **'pure'**. He is talking now about their
moral characters. That which is right is that which is in keeping
with God's law. That which is pure is that which is free from
any blemish or corruption. The Lord Jesus Christ had taught
the same things. He said that his followers should act like salt
and light in the world (Matt. 5:13-16).[3]

Finally, the last couplet, **'whatever is lovely, whatever is
admirable,'** has to do with the way they appear to others.
These are qualities that affect other people. The word 'lovely'
can be translated 'winsome'. The Lord wants us to act in ways
which draw out love in other people. Paul has already described this kind of admirable behaviour when he exhorted the
Philippians to 'Do everything without complaining or arguing, so that you may become blameless and pure, children of
God without fault in a crooked and depraved generation'
(2:14-15).

After naming all these virtues he says that they should think
about these wonderful things. Obviously this is not an exhaus-
tive list, so the apostle adds, **'If anything is excellent or
praiseworthy — think about such things'** (4:8).

If anyone reading this book does not know what kind of
things to meditate on, Paul gives some guidance here. He is
saying that we should think about things that are excellent and
praiseworthy. These are the good, wholesome matters which
should occupy our minds, and lead us into healthy thinking.
But so often our minds dwell on the opposite of these virtues.
If every member of the church followed these guidelines, none
of us would be guilty of unkindly criticizing any of our fellow
believers. And if we all dwelt on that which is excellent and
praiseworthy, none of us would lose our temper with anyone

else. Churches would be wonderful places if everyone was to keep thinking on these good things which Paul lists here.

However, thinking about the right things is not enough; we must also live in the right way.

## Right living

We can live aright when we think rightly. If we fail to think on the kind of things mentioned in this list, then we are never going to know the presence of the God of peace. Nor are we going to be very much use to the people living around us who are not Christians.

However, Paul does not just give us advice on how to live and then say, 'Get on with it.' He gives us a further piece of guidance: **'Whatever you have learned or received or heard from me, or seen in me — put it into practice'** (4:9). On the face of it, this piece of advice appears to contradict Paul's teaching that we should all be humble. He tells them, 'Look at me. Follow the example I have set you.' But the apostle is not bragging about his own importance; he is saying that if we are to experience the presence of the God of peace, then we are required to model ourselves on the way Paul lived.

But Paul was shut up in prison. What good would it have done the Philippians to copy him? Did he mean that they too should get themselves arrested and imprisoned? Of course not. He meant that they were to have the same attitude as he had. If he could experience the peace of God as a prisoner, how much more would the Philippians be able to do so in the freedom they enjoyed![4] He says, 'I want you to look at me and notice how I live my life.' Or we could put it like this: 'What it is that drives me along? Who is the one person who is my guiding principle for everything I think and do?' When Paul wrote in this way they knew that it was the Lord Jesus Christ and his honour which controlled every aspect of Paul's life. He has already told them, 'For to me, to live is Christ and to die is gain' (1:21).

These people had met Paul. He had spent time with them in their church; indeed, he had been involved in founding it. They had also met many people who had spent a great deal of time in Paul's company, such as Timothy and Epaphroditus. So Paul is saying to them in this verse what he has already said in 3:17: 'Join with others in following my example, brothers, and take note of those who live according to the pattern we gave you.' In other words he is saying, 'Whatever you have learned about me — copy it. Whatever you have received from me — follow it. Whatever you have heard from me — pass it on to others. And whatever you have seen in me — imitate it.'

What does this mean for us today, who have never met Paul, heard him preach, or had the opportunity to observe at first hand his manner of life? When the apostle told the Philippians to copy him he meant, 'Live like me, because I am seeking to live like Christ.' Paul's great model was the Lord Jesus Christ himself. This is described so beautifully in the opening verses of chapter 2 of this letter: 'Your attitude should be the same as that of Christ Jesus' (2:5). Or, as the Authorized Version puts it, 'Let this mind be in you, which was also in Christ Jesus.' We should strive to have the mind of Christ and to live as he lived. If we do so, then we shall truly be blessed.


**Right blessings**

How can we know that we are thinking right things and doing right things? We can do so when we have the God of peace as our God. **'The God of peace'** is one of Paul's favourite descriptions of God. He uses it towards the end of many of his epistles (Rom. 15:33; 16:20; 1 Cor. 14:33; 2 Cor. 13:11; Phil. 4:9; cf. 2 Thess. 3:16).

However, we must be careful here. Although God never gives us his inner peace about anything that is wrong, we should still be on our guard because sometimes we can deceive ourselves into a false sense of peace. This happened in Jeremiah's time when the false prophets told the people not to worry about anything, but Jeremiah told them that these prophets were only dressing the wound of God's people as though it were not serious. They were saying, '"Peace, peace" ... when there is no peace' (Jer. 6:14).

We can only experience the genuine peace of God when we know that we are right with him. Only those who have been born again, and are truly the children of God, can experience this peace. Those who are thinking right things and doing right actions are the ones who know, for certain, the presence of the God of peace.

When we rejoice in the Lord and pray aright, then the peace of God will guard our hearts and minds (4:7), and the God of peace, who provides everything we need for life and eternity, will guide us into his ways.

# 20.
# The secret of contentment

*Please read Philippians 4:10-13*

There is a great lack of contentment in the world today, and this attitude so often begins to spill over into the church. Young people appear to get bored very easily, even though they have so many more things to occupy them than there were in former days. Some older people, too, complain because they think the government should give them a larger pension, because they did so much for the country when they were younger. There is a great deal of discontent about among all sorts of people, and this air of dissatisfaction is catching.

When people are not satisfied with their wages, or their conditions of employment, they want to go on strike. When tenants are unhappy with their council houses, they bombard the authorities with demands for improvements. And when a person thinks that he has not received sufficient attention from his doctor he complains to the Health Commission. There are so many people who are discontented; they seem to be constantly complaining about something or other.

But if there was anyone who had just cause to complain, it was Paul. He was in prison for no justifiable reason. He was prevented from doing the work that God had called him to do, and he was unable to visit the churches who meant so much to him. However, instead of grumbling, he said, **'I rejoice greatly in the Lord'** (4:10). How could he say that when he was in such trouble? What was it that made him so cheerful, when he had to put up with so much discomfort? It was the fact that he had learned the secret of contentment.

In this chapter we can learn from Paul about the secret of contentment. There are at least three lessons that we can draw from what he tells us about his situation. Firstly, we ought to be grateful for what we have. Secondly, we should be content with our situation. Thirdly, we ought to be confident in the source of our strength.

## Gratitude for what we receive

Despite all of his discomfort, Paul was grateful for the little he did have. He had his Lord — and he was right there with him in his prison cell. Christ was very precious to the apostle. He had rescued him from his self-righteousness and his dependence upon religious observances. He had appointed him as his apostle, or messenger, to the Gentiles; and not even the cruellest of jailers could take the Lord away from him.

Secondly, he had many happy memories of his friends at Philippi. Nothing could deprive him of the joy he experienced whenever he remembered them and prayed for them (1:3-4). He was encouraged because he knew that the believers over there in Macedonia were concerned about him. He knew that they were praying for him and, on top of all their other kindness to him, they had sent him a gift (4:18).

Paul was very pleased to receive this gift. He uses a horticultural term to express his delight when he says, **'I rejoice greatly in the Lord that at last you have renewed your concern for me'** (4:10). The Greek word means, 'Your concern for me has bloomed again' (see Ezek. 17:24).[1]

When we first glance at this verse it may seem as if Paul was exasperated because their gift had taken a long time to reach him. However, when he says, 'At last you have renewed your concern for me,' he does not mean that he was hurt by the delay. He knew that there was some good reason why this gift had taken so long to reach him. It is possible that it had taken the Philippians a long time to save up the money (assuming that the gift was one of cash). It may have been that no reliable messenger could be found to take the present to Paul, but it is more likely that the delay was caused because the Philippian believers did not know where the apostle was being held as a prisoner.

Paul did not want to give the impression that he thought the believers were slow in helping him. In other places he commends these Macedonian Christians (i.e. the churches at Thessalonica and Philippi) most highly for their generosity in sustaining his ministry through their financial support. He uses the example of their generosity to encourage the church at Corinth to give to the work of the Lord. He writes to them, 'Now, brothers, we want you to know about the grace that God has given the Macedonian churches. Out of the most severe trial, their overflowing joy and their extreme poverty welled up in rich generosity' (2 Cor. 8:1-2).

Let us break away from this story for a moment. If a believer supports the Lord's work, that gift should not be despised, however small it might be. A missionary working in some far-flung part of the world, who felt very neglected by those at home, would be grateful to receive even the smallest gift of money towards his (or her) work. The money may be too little to buy very much food, but it does show the love which the friends back at home have for the Christian worker. It is the attitude with which a gift is made that counts more than anything else.

There was an occasion when Jesus was sitting with his disciples opposite the place where people put in their offerings for the temple. As they watched, they saw many rich people throwing in large amounts of money. (They threw the money into the treasury in such a way that everyone could see how much they were giving.) Then a very poor widow came and put in two very small copper coins, worth only a fraction of a penny (which was not very much money at all). Jesus told his disciples, 'I tell you the truth, this poor widow has put more into the treasury than all the others.' He explained what he meant by saying, 'They all gave out of their wealth; but she, out of her poverty, put in everything — all she had to live on' (Mark 12:43,44).

That is what true sacrificial giving is like. It is not how much money you give to the Lord's work that matters. It is how much you have left over for yourself after you have given, and the attitude with which you gave it, that counts with God.

## Contentment with our situation

Paul, back in his prison, was rejoicing over the gift which the Philippians had sent to him. When he says, **'I am not saying this because I am in need'** (4:11), what he really means is: 'I am not rejoicing *just* because I am in need.' Did he mean that he was ungrateful for the gift which they had sent him? Of course not. When he said, 'I rejoice greatly in the Lord,' he was expressing his appreciation for their gift, but he was even more full of joy because he knew that every good and perfect gift comes from God (see James 1:17).

Although he was glad of the gift, he wanted his readers to know that his happiness did not depend upon his circumstances. He tells them, **'I have learned to be content whatever the circumstances'** (4:11). When he said that his circumstances did not dictate how he felt, did he mean that he was living in some kind of trance which had taken him out of the pain of this world? Was it that he had come under the influence of the pagan Stoic philosophers of those days who claimed that they had learned the secret of being self-sufficient and were, therefore, able to set themselves apart from everything that happened around them?[2]

He was not saying any of these things, nor had he discovered any other system for coping with trials. He meant that he was content because he had been set free from relying on mere 'things' for his satisfaction. The Lord himself said, 'A man's life does not consist in the abundance of his possessions' (Luke 12:15). Paul had learned to cast the whole of his life upon Christ and to trust him for each and every one of his needs (see 4:19).

He lived a contented life, whether he had a huge amount of material things, or whether he was deprived of the basic necessities of life. He had learned how to cope even when he had very few material possessions. This was because he knew that the Lord would always supply his basic needs. In the years since he had found Christ as his Saviour the apostle had proved the truth of the psalmist's words: 'I have never seen the righteous forsaken or their children begging bread' (Ps. 37:25). He had found that to be the case in his own experience. He had been imprisoned many times; he had been flogged, stoned and shipwrecked. He had known hunger and thirst and had often been cold and naked. Yet, throughout all these conditions, he had found out that his God met all his needs (see 2 Cor. 11; 12).

Not only had he been able to cope when he had very few possessions, he had also learned to deal with the dangers of prosperity. It seems a strange thing to say, but in some ways it is harder to stick to our Christian faith when things are going well with us than when we are in trouble. Many a believer has stumbled because he had too many of this life's goods. One day King David stayed at home while his army went to war, and he sunk back in the luxury of his lovely palace. It was then that his eyes strayed to another man's wife, Bathsheba (2 Sam. 11:1-5). Because he had plenty of time on his hands and was prosperous, he fell into grievous sin — and afterwards suffered for it.

There have been many instances in the history of Britain, too, of people who have made a thorough mess of their lives because they have acted selfishly and lived debauched lives. In his early years, as Prince of Wales, King George IV gorged himself on every pleasure imaginable. It is said that he was even rolling drunk when he took his wedding vows.

Paul knew all about every kind of moral and physical danger, but he had learned how to rise above the temptations of living in plenty or in want. That is what he means when he writes, **'I have learned the secret of being content in any and every situation'** (4:12). Whatever happened to him, he was never going to complain. He was satisfied, whatever his situation.

It ought to be the same for us. If we are going to learn the secret of contentment, then we must not seek satisfaction in anything that the world offers us. Some people turn for comfort to alcohol, drugs, or worldly pleasure when things go against them. They then discover, in the end, that none of these things satisfies the deepest needs of anyone. The believer should learn the sentiment of the old hymn which says,

O Christ, in thee my soul hath found,
And found in thee alone,
The peace, the joy I sought so long,
The bliss till now unknown.

Now none but Christ can satisfy —
None other name for me!
There's love and life and lasting joy,
Lord Jesus, found in thee.[3]

We must be content with Christ, and lean on no one else. Charles Wesley wrote,

Thou, O Christ, art all I want;
All in all in thee I find;
Raise the fallen, cheer the faint,
Heal the sick, and lead the blind.[4]


## Confidence in the source of our strength

Paul ends this paragraph by making this great assertion: **'I can do everything through him who gives me strength'** (4:13). Many people long to be able to say, 'I can do everything.' If that was true for them, then nothing would be out of their reach. They would be hailed as great and powerful people.

But Paul is not claiming here to be a popular wonder-worker. He means, 'I can do everything provided God wants me to do it.' That was the secret of his contentment. He could live knowing the strength of God was flowing through him, enabling him to carry out God's will. That was all he wanted to do.

To understand what the apostle is saying we must take this verse in connection with the two previous ones. He knew that, whatever God called him to pass through, the Lord would give him the strength to bear a good witness to him in it. This was because he knew that God's grace was sufficient for him in every situation. Even when he was very weak, physically or emotionally, he knew that Christ's power was resting upon him. 'For Christ's sake,' he could say, 'I delight in weaknesses, in insults, in hardships, in persecutions, in difficulties. For when I am weak, then I am strong' (2 Cor. 12:9-10).

Is the guiding principle of our lives that we want to please God? The writer to the Hebrews tells us that 'Without faith it is impossible to please God, because anyone who comes to him must believe that he exists and that he rewards those who earnestly seek him' (Heb. 11:6).

The secret of living a contented life is to live trusting in God and seeking to please him in everything.

# 21.
# Support God's work

*Please read Philippians 4:14-23*

There are so very many people in need in the world today that we scarcely know how to help them. One of the most practical ways is to give towards their financial support; in particular we should help those who are serving the Lord. All those who have left home and loved ones to go and take the message of the gospel to needy areas require the help of others. Those who have only travelled a few hundred miles to a distant area of the country for the sake of the gospel are as much in need of our prayers and interest as those who have gone to far distant parts of the world to take the message of salvation. However, we should remember that missionaries have given up a great deal to go overseas and take the good news of salvation to others, and they can only do that efficiently if they receive adequate support from people in their homelands.

Paul had endured much persecution as he travelled around the Roman Empire seeking to win men and women for Christ, and establishing churches in every place. He had done his best to support himself through his tent-making, but this ate into the time he wanted to spend teaching people about the Christian faith. So the greater the amount of financial support he received from established churches, the less time he needed to devote to earning his living, and the more hours he could give to reaching out to others with the good news of salvation in

Christ Jesus. We can see, then, how thankful he was that his friends in Macedonia, and particularly at Philippi, had sent many gifts to enable him to spend a greater proportion of his time in the Lord's work.

## Our giving blesses others

Whenever a missionary receives a gift from a friend at home, he (or she) is blessed through it. It does not have to be a huge gift. Even the smallest amount of money tells the worker that his friends at home are standing with him in his work. He is reminded that he is not working alone. Naturally, he is aware that the Lord is with him, but a present from home assures him that his friends are supporting him in all his efforts to work for the Lord.

There is nothing like a practical expression of support to encourage someone in his work. Missionaries can be very lonely, even though work overseas may sometimes seem glamorous and exciting to us. There must be many, many times when a missionary lies down at night, utterly exhausted and demoralized, thinking that no one understands the pressures he is undergoing.

We can be sure too that the devil will try to tell him that no one cares either. He will say to the Lord's servant, 'It's all right for the people in your home church. They are safe at home living in their comfortable houses and sleeping in their warm beds. They don't really care what you are going through. They are only salving their consciences by sending you a mere pittance from time to time. They think then that they have done their duty.'

Paul must have felt rather like that on many occasions, but he knew that his friends at home could imagine the effect his imprisonment was having on him. So he wanted to encourage them and thank them for their gifts towards his work. He tells the Corinthians that 'God loves a cheerful giver' (2 Cor. 9:7). and here he writes to the Philippians, **'It was good of you to share my troubles'** (4:14). He knew that the Philippians sympathized with him when things were going badly, and they were filled with joy when his efforts met with great success.

The apostle was greatly blessed by the gifts which were sent by the Philippians and by the love which lay behind each of them. The believers at Philippi had started sending money to Paul when they were still a very new church — even though they probably had not received much guidance on how they should function. They did not say, 'Give us time to get on our feet. We will support you when we have saved up a good balance at the bank.' From the earliest days of their acquaintance with the gospel, they gave more than any other church to the support of Paul's work of spreading the good news. Even when the apostle had moved on to Thessalonica (some eighty miles to the west of Philippi), they continued to send their money for his support. Now, about ten years later, they were still sending gifts — this time by the hand of Epaphroditus.

But the value of their giving was not measured in comparison with the gifts which others sent. They did not ask Paul for a scale of charges so that they could work out how much they ought to contribute to his work (in the way that some Christian groups give guidance to their member churches). Nor did they say, 'What is the going rate of giving for a church of our size and financial make-up?' They gave generously, regardless of how much, or how little, other churches gave to Paul. In fact it seems that, certainly at this time, only the Philippians sent the apostle any gifts to sustain him in his trials. It was for this reason that Paul said that it was good of them to share in his troubles (4:14).

One of the things that we can learn from this passage is that giving to mission must be organized. This is where a good church treasurer is a real 'treasure'. The elders should be occupied with other matters, such as prayer, study and ministering to the spiritual needs of the people. They should not have to spend their time dealing with financial issues. It is in these matters that you need a good, sanctified, business head. That seems to be what the Philippians did possess.

Perhaps that great and gracious businesswoman Lydia was behind all of this systematic giving. Certainly Paul describes their giving in accounting terms. He talks about **'the matter of giving and receiving'** (4:15). That suggests the credit and debit sides of an accounts ledger. He has also used the same terminology in 3:7, where he mentioned profit and loss. So he adds, **'Not that I am looking for a gift, but I am looking for what may be credited to your account'** (4:17). In other words, he is saying that he is encouraged by their gifts because he knows that God will mark their generosity down in his heavenly accounts ledger to their credit.

Finally, he tells them, **'I have received full payment and even more; I am amply supplied'** (4:18). This is like saying, 'Here is the receipt which is stamped, "Paid in full".' In fact, it had not just been paid in full, but over and above the sum due — the payment had been made in abundance!

## Our giving enriches us

Another reason why Paul was encouraged by their gifts was because he knew that the Christians at Philippi would be blessed through their generosity. The Lord himself said, 'It is more blessed to give than to receive' (Acts 20:35). It is a sign of maturity when we have that attitude. When we were little children we became very excited at Christmas, and could hardly wait to open our presents to see what we had been given, but when we grew a little older we discovered great joy in giving to others, and seeing their faces light up when they opened the parcels we had given them.

It is the same in the Lord's work. Of course, we should never give a gift primarily in the hope of receiving a blessing as a result of doing so. That would be pure selfishness, which is one of the attitudes which Paul has been trying to discourage all through this letter. Each of us should examine our motives for giving to others. We should never give just because others are giving and we would be shown up by not doing the same. Neither should we give solely because we know that as Christians we are obliged to give to others. And we should certainly never give merely because we know that God is going to bless us because we do so.

However, it is a fact that Paul promises these Philippian Christians that **'My God will meet all your needs'** (4:19). This is a tremendous claim for the apostle to make. How could he do such a thing? He could have tried to promise that he would give them support, but what right had he to promise that his God would not just help them, but would actually supply all of their needs?

He could say such a thing because he knew that his God was rich in blessings. He never forgot all that God had done for him. He, the chief of sinners, had received so much from God and he knew that the Lord would also do the same for all true believers. That means that Paul was not only confident that his God would supply the needs of the members of the Philippian church in those days. It means that the same God — for he is eternal — is still active today, and he will supply each and every one of our needs too, if we truly belong to him.

These words hung over my bed when I was a child and I have never forgotten them. There were many occasions when I had lain awake at night, or in the early morning, and stared at the Gothic-style lettering of those words, coloured in blue, red and gold and set in the heavy gilded picture frame. In my early years I could not read them, but later I knew what they meant and it could be said that I have grown up with that text. The meaning of it has never left me. I know that it is true and I am certain that my God will supply all my needs.

I know that it is true, not only because I believe what God says, but because I have experienced the Lord's help so many times in my life. On one occasion I received a huge telephone bill, that was not of my making, and I did not know how I could pay it. But God met that bill through the generosity of one of his servants. On another occasion my car broke down and I needed a new engine costing far, far more than I had in the bank, or could ever hope to work for. But God supplied my need and a Christian friend paid for that also. I can testify that this is true; God supplied my every need.

What a great comfort this truth is to God's people! If we belong to him, then we know that we shall never be forsaken. Everything that we need for our physical and spiritual welfare will be supplied by the Lord. Just as Paul's needs had been met by his friends at Philippi, so the Philippians' needs would be met by Paul's God. And our needs too will be met out of the abundance of God's riches.

However, we must be careful here. Paul's God promises to supply our needs. He does not promise to supply our 'greeds'. Neither does he promise to supply all of our wants. But everything that we need for our spiritual and physical well-being, the Lord promises to give us.

Where does God obtain this provision to meet our needs? Out of the abundance of his riches. He does not say that he will give to us out of his riches. That is what a millionaire might do when he gives us a trifling amount, still leaving much for himself. God gives to us **'according to his glorious riches'** (4:19). That means that he gives to us in proportion to his infinite resources. When we became Christians we were incorporated 'in Christ Jesus' (see 1:1). We were united to our

Saviour in a very real and living way. Therefore, because God gave up his own dear Son to die for us on the cross, along with this gift of himself, he will graciously give us all things (Rom. 8:32).

A second thing that we must be careful about is to remember that because the Lord promises to supply all of our needs, that does not mean that we can just sit back and wait for him to give us all these blessings. Laziness is never encouraged in the Lord's servants. Paul gave the Thessalonians this rule: 'If a man will not work, he shall not eat' (2 Thess. 3:10).

People who say they live by faith should remember this teaching. I met someone once, in Athens, who said that he had been sent by the Lord to take the gospel throughout Africa and the Middle East (without being sent out by a church, or even having the backing of a home church). He acted as though he thought that the believers in the Greek church where he was staying should automatically provide him and his wife with food and clothing, while neither of them did anything to help themselves. The Christians in that local church were very generous, but my wife and I were ashamed that an Englishman should expect hard-working, honest Christian people to give food and money (which they could ill afford) to these people who claimed to be missionaries, when in fact they were scroungers who did nothing to help themselves.

Finally, we read that these riches are 'glorious' (4:19). Paul was not just writing about material blessings.[1] He was talking about the riches which are in glory, where one day we shall be with our Lord and remain for ever.

## Our giving pleases God

The greatest motivation for all of us to give to others, and so help them in their work of spreading the gospel, is the fact that it pleases God (4:18). Paul tells us that our gifts for the Lord's work are like a fragrant offering to God. In the Old Testament the priests did not just offer sacrifices to atone for the sins of the people. They offered sacrifices of thanksgiving as well (see Lev. 7:12-15). This means that when we give anything at all to further God's work that gift will be accepted by God as a fragrant offering.

I have some very lovely, sweet-smelling roses in my garden and I look forward each year for Gertrude Jekyll, Abraham Darby and Margaret Merril to bloom. When the first buds open, I plunge my nose deeply into them and drink in the gorgeous aroma of their perfume. Their lovely scent gives me tremendous pleasure. It is the same when we give to the work of the Lord. Our gifts, and the love behind them, ascend up to God like a fragrant offering, but one which is far more pleasing to God than the very best of flowers. God is well-pleased when we support his work by prayer, interest and practical giving.

Our love to God and to others is just like a fragrant offering to the Lord. The apostle tells the Ephesians that 'just as Christ loved us and gave himself up for us as a fragrant offering and sacrifice to God,' so we should 'live a life of love' (Eph. 5:2). When the ark finally settled and Noah and his family stepped out onto dry land, one of the first things that Noah did was to build an altar to the Lord. Then he took some of the clean birds and sacrificed burnt offerings on the altar. The effect of that was that 'The Lord smelled the pleasing aroma and said in his heart, "Never again will I curse the ground"' (Gen. 8:21).

'When Christians take note of Christian needs and extend themselves in generous accommodation to other Christians, it is, for God, the burnt offering all over again, and he delights to accept it.'[2] This generous attitude of giving to others brings glory to God's name. The thought leads Paul to burst out with one of his great doxologies of praise to God: **'To our God and Father be glory for ever and ever. Amen'** (4:20).

As Paul ends this lovely letter, he comes full circle and emphasizes once again the oneness of God's people. He had addressed the letter 'to all the saints in Christ Jesus at Philippi' (1:1), and then added the words: 'together with the overseers and deacons'. This letter was addressed in the first place, not to the leaders, but to 'all the saints'. So Paul ends this epistle the same way. He says, **'Greet all the saints in Christ Jesus'** (4:21). He does not single out one leader or group of leaders. He just writes, 'Greet all the saints.'

He also sends greetings from **'all the saints'** where he was at the time. Now he does single out some. First, he says, **'The brothers who are with me send greetings'** (4:21). He is probably referring to his fellow prisoners and travellers, as opposed to those who lived permanently in Rome. Among these would have been Timothy and perhaps Luke. The second group of saints that the apostle singles out are **'those who belong to Cæsar's household'** (4:22). He does not mean that Cæsar's relatives sent their greetings (unless any of them were believers), but is almost certainly referring to those who worked in the palace and had become Christians (see 1:13). They would have belonged to the imperial civil service, which had members all over the world.[3]

Finally, Paul concludes this letter as he began it. In the opening verses he had wished them, 'Grace and peace ... from God our Father and the Lord Jesus Christ' (1:2). Now he ends this epistle, as he does so many of his letters, with: **'The grace of the Lord Jesus Christ be with your spirit. Amen'** (4:23). In other words, as one commentator put it, 'God will deal graciously with each of those who turn to him and make such Christians gracious to each other.'[4]

# Notes

### Chapter 1 — Joyful people
1. William Hendriksen, *The Epistle to the Philippians,* Banner of Truth Trust, 1963, p.6.
2. As above, p.43.
3. Ralph Martin, *Philippians,* IVP, 1959, p.59.

### Chapter 2 — Joyful memories
1. Warren Wiersbe, *Be Joyful,* Scripture Press, 1984, p.29.
2. Hendriksen, *Philippians,* p.53.

### Chapter 3 — Genuine longing
1. W. E. Vine, *An Expository Dictionary of New Testament Words,* Oliphants, 1940, vol. III, p.21.
2. Charles Swindoll, *Laugh Again,* Insight for Living, 1992, p.15.
3. Wiersbe, *Be Joyful,* p.35.

### Chapter 4 — The preaching of Christ
1. Wiersbe, *Be Joyful,* p.37.
2. Hendriksen, *Philippians,* p.69.
3. As above, p.71.
4. See Peter T. O'Brien, *The Epistle to the Philippians,* Eerdmans, 1991, p.98.

### Chapter 5 — A difficult choice
1. Ivor H. Evans, *Brewer's Dictionary of Phrase and Fable,* Cassell, 1989, p.329.
2. John Blanchard, *Gathered Gold,* Evangelical Press, 1984, pp.227, 228.
3. Hywel R. Jones, *Philippians,* Christian Focus Publications, 1993, p.43.
4. Martin, *Philippians,* p.75.
5. Hendriksen, *Philippians,* p.76.
6. Wiersbe, *Be Joyful,* pp.45-6.

### Chapter 6 — Live worthily
1. Wiersbe, *Be Joyful,* p.50.
2. An example of this kind of thinking is recorded in *The Mystery of Salvation,* a

report by the Church of England's doctrine commission published in January 1996. *The Times* reported that this declared that hell is the final and irrevocable 'choosing of that which is opposed to God so completely and so absolutely that the only end of life is total non-being' (*The Times*, 11 January 1996).
3. Jones, *Philippians*, p.55.

### Chapter 7 — How to please your pastor
1. Martin, *Philippians*, p.91.
2. *NIV Study Bible*, p.1771.
3. *Collins Concise Dictionary*, p.409.
4. John F. Walvoord, *Philippians, Triumph in Christ*, Moody Press, 1971, p.50.
5. Hendriksen, *Philippians*, pp.97-8.
6. John Blanchard, *More Gathered Gold*, Evangelical Press, 1986, p.160.
7. J. B. Lightfoot, *Philippians*, Crossway Classic Commentaries, ed. Alister McGrath and J. I. Packer, 1994, p.123.

### Chapter 8 — Imitate Jesus the Lord
1. O'Brien, *Philippians*, 1991, p.216.
2. See James Montgomery Boice, *Foundations of the Christian Faith*, IVP, 1986, pp.268-9.
3. From the hymn, 'And can it be that I should gain...?', no. 566 in *Grace Hymns*.
4. O'Brien, *Philippians*, p.218.
5. As above, p.268.
6. See Hendriksen, *Philippians*, p.109.
7. J. A. Motyer, *The Richness of Christ*, IVP, 1966, p.74.
8. Walvoord, *Philippians, Triumph in Christ*, p.58.
9. Jones, *Philippians*, p.77.

### Chapter 9 — Shine brightly
1. Hendriksen, *Philippians*, p.120.
2. Moisés Silva, *Philippians*, Baker Book House, 1992, pp.142-3.
3. William Barclay, *The Daily Study Bible; The Letters to the Philippians, Colossians and Thessalonians*, St Andrew Press, 1975, p.44.
4. Motyer, *The Richness of Christ*, p.91.

### Chapter 10 — Serve faithfully
1. D. Martyn Lloyd-Jones, *The Life of Joy*, Hodder & Stoughton, 1993, p.224.
2. This was written in a personal letter from my good friend, Mrs Irene Simmonds of Crowthorne.
3. Silva, *Philippians*, p.156.
4. Lloyd-Jones, *The Life of Joy*, p.228.

### Chapter 11 — Care passionately
1. Hendriksen, *Philippians*, p.138.
2. Barclay, *Daily Study Bible*, p.48.
3. Martin, *Philippians*, p.133.
4. See Lloyd-Jones, *The Life of Joy*, pp.230-31.

### Chapter 12 — Beware of religion!
1. Lightfoot, *Philippians*, p.158.
2. Silva, *Philippians*, p.169.
3. Motyer, *The Richness of Christ*, p.116.
4. Silva, *Philippians*, p.170.
5. Wiersbe, *Be Joyful*, p.98.

### Chapter 13 — Four plus three equals a minus
1. Hendriksen, *Philippians*, p.156.
2. As above, p.161.
3. Barclay, *Daily Study Bible*, p.58.
4. Jones, *Philippians*, p.116.
5. Barclay, *Daily Study Bible*, p.59.
6. Jones, *Philippians*, p.117.
7. Silva, *Philippians*, p.174.
8. Hendriksen, *Philippians*, p.162.

### Chapter 14 — Knowing Christ personally
1. Elisabeth Eliot, *The Shadow of the Almighty*, Hodder & Stoughton, 1958, p.19.
2. Lightfoot, *Philippians*, p.163.
3. See Hendriksen, *Philippians*, p.166.
4. This version of Zinzendorf's hymn is No. 344 in *Hymns of Faith*. However, No. 103 gives us another, possibly older, version:

> Jesus, thy blood and righteousness
> My beauty are, my glorious dress;
> 'Midst flaming worlds, in these arrayed,
> With joy shall I lift up my head.

5. D. Martyn Lloyd-Jones, *The Life of Peace*, Hodder & Stoughton, 1993, p.68.
6. Hymn by E. E. Hewitt, No. 394 in *Redemption Hymnal*.

### Chapter 15 — Pressing onwards
1. Jones, *Philippians*, p.130.
2. Swindoll, *Laugh Again*, p.74.

### Chapter 16 — Keep your eyes open
1. John Owen, *Apostasy from the Gospel*, ed. R. J. K. Law, Banner of Truth Trust, 1992, p.105.
2. Barclay, *Daily Study Bible*, p.69.

### Chapter 17 — Internal conflict: the great enemy of the church
1. Owen, *Apostasy from the Gospel*, p.137.
2. Motyer, *The Richness of Christ*, p.163.
3. Barclay, *Daily Study Bible*, p.71.
4. See Lloyd-Jones, *The Life of Peace*, p.134.
5. Barclay, *Daily Study Bible*, p.70.

6. Silva, *Philippians,* p.221.
7. Jones, *Philippians,* p.141.

### Chapter 18 — God's cure for worry
1. Lloyd-Jones, *The Life of Peace,* p.168.
2. Wiersbe, *Be Joyful,* pp.131-2.
3. Silva, *Philippians,* p.224.
4. Quoted by Martin, *Philippians,* p.168.
5. Swindoll, *Laugh Again,* p.99.
6. The second verse of the hymn which starts, 'Come, my soul, thy suit prepare. Jesus loves to answer prayer...' (Hymn no. 454 in *Hymns of Faith* and also found in many other books).
7. Hendriksen, *Philippians,* p.196.

### Chapter 19 — Be good citizens
1. Blanchard, *Gathered Gold,* p.313.
2. Walvoord, *Philippians, Triumph in Christ,* p.109.
3. Jones, *Philippians,* p.148.
4. Walvoord, *Philippians, Triumph in Christ,* p.110.

### Chapter 20 — The secret of contentment
1. Martin, *Philippians,* p.175.
2. Motyer, *The Richness of Christ,* p.176.
3. No. 853 in Sankey's *Sacred Songs and Solos.*
4. From the hymn 'Jesus, Lover of my Soul', no. 303 in Gadsby's hymn-book.

### Chapter 21 — Support God's work
1. Lightfoot, *Philippians,* p.184.
2. Motyer, *The Richness of Christ,* p.175.
3. Barclay, *Daily Study Bible,* p.87.
4. Jones, *Philippians,* p.159.